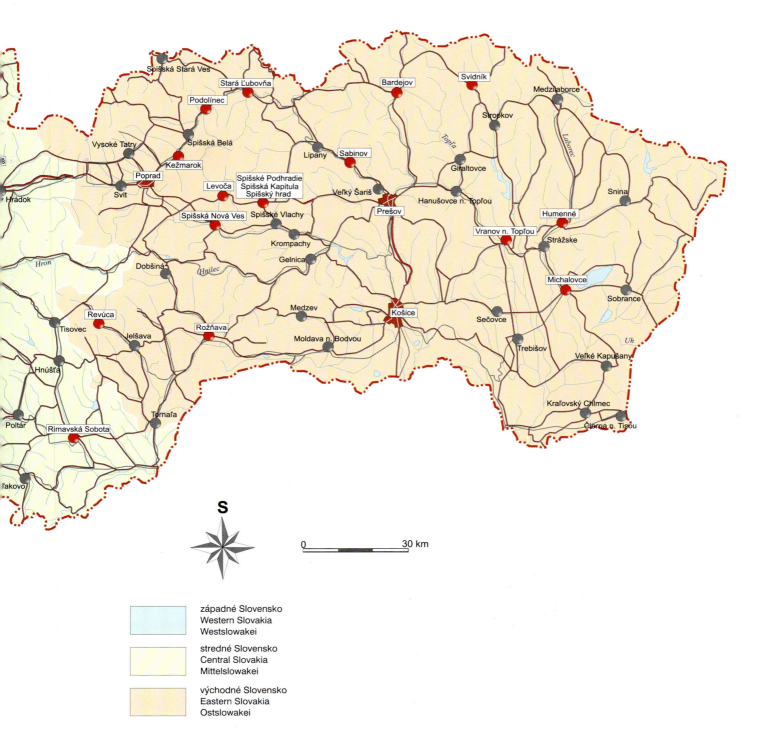

S

0   30 km

západné Slovensko
Western Slovakia
Westslowakei

stredné Slovensko
Central Slovakia
Mittelslowakei

východné Slovensko
Eastern Slovakia
Ostslowakei

55
Loveliest
Places
in SLOVAKIA

Jozef Leikert

Alexander Vojček

55

Loveliest Places

in SLOVAKIA

Príroda

Text © doc. PhDr. Jozef Leikert, PhD., 2007
Photos © Alexander Vojček 2007
English edition © Vydavateľstvo Príroda, s. r. o., Bratislava 2007
Translation © Tomáš Štorcel and Terence Moran, 2007

Graphic layout and cover: Jozef Vysoký

First edition
Published 2007 by Vydavateľstvo Príroda, s. r. o., Bratislava
Responsible editor Magdaléna Belanová
Technical editor Darina Mrláková
Printed by Polygraf print, s. r. o., Prešov
Issue No. 8555

64-002-07

ISBN 978-80-07-01522-7

This book is available to be bought in all good bookshops all around Slovakia.
Also, you are welcome to order it by mail at the following address:
Vydavateľstvo Príroda, s. r. o., Koceľova 17, 821 08 Bratislava 2
Or, by phone: 02/55 42 51 60
Or, via e-mail: priroda@priroda.sk

www.priroda.sk

CONTENTS

IM IAHR CHRISTI 174[.]
IST DIESE RATHSTEIN BV[.]
IETZIGE V. NACHCOMEN[.]
FVNDIERET WORDEN
IN RICH: AMT IAC. SPVLLER[.]
VORMVNDT AND FRÖLIC[H.]
IVR. TOB. ROXER. IOH. GVN[.]
IOH. PISCHL. IOH. GROS[.]
IOH. REIS. IOH. 24[.]
DAN. SCVETI. IOH. FRO[.]
ISRA. SCHOLL. IAC. SA[.]
AND. LVDROFF.SC. MAR[.]
IAC. STEPHANI. DAN[.]
PAVL. PE.SCH[.]
IOH BA[.]

INTRODUCTION

Ernest Hemingway once said that the world is a lovely place and that it's worth living in. No need to paraphrase his words - we can say that Slovakia is a country worth living in, or at least visiting.

The Gods have been generous to this small country in the heart of Europe. The small piece of land between the Danube and the Tatra Mountains was given so much beauty, only a few countries elsewhere in the world can match. They bestowed upon it lovely mountains, magnificent rivers, picturesque valleys and fertile lowlands. Then they sent people there - people not only wise and hardworking, but also modest, warm-hearted and virtuous. Those early residents began to build the first dwellings here, then castles, forts, chateaux, churches, extending to villages, towns and then later cities. They built the foundations of a valuable heritage that's now admired by more and more visitors from all around the world.

Although they later found themselves on the crossroads of different spiritual cultures, they still had the power to raise their own culture, history - so singular and irreplaceable. Kings, rulers, emperors, the rich, but also the poor and common people left here indelible traces, joining their wit and skilfulness, as well as admirable harmony between man and nature.

Archaeological findings in Slovakia today bear witness to urbanisation, as well as to numerous contacts with both close and faraway countries. Archaeological research, still vibrant nowadays, has been turning up new secrets from the history of the country and life here centuries ago, piecing together the endless mosaic of people's lives in the past. This is especially thanks to getting more and more familiar with the cultural sights and natural treasures of Slovakia.

The book that you're holding in your hands right now offers you taking a road to the loveliest sights and exceptionalities of 55 Slovak towns and cities. It's not meant to be an encyclopaedia or a book of history and geography. Rather, it's an invitation for you to visit the most beautiful spots and the most interesting corners in Slovakia. By words and pictures it attempts to create an atmosphere of the past and the present, tracing the history of Slovakia and Slovaks. It gives you an account of selected unique places in the country, unusual historical sights and precious cultural highlights, which could spark sufficient interest to visit.

We believe that this book will serve as a charm in the bracelet of your wanderlust, enticing you to look around the best of what such a lovely country as Slovakia has to offer. It's a beautiful country, definitely worthy of a visit and your admiration.

BRATISLAVA

The Hospitable Royal City

Only a few European towns have a reputation of having been a coronation town for almost three hundred years. In Bratislava, eleven kings and eight queens (including popular Empress Maria Theresé) were crowned here in the past. Little wonder then that kings and queens were always very partial towards the town upon the Danube River.

As a town and city, Bratislava has a history dating back 2,000 years to Celtic times. The Celtic tribes largely influenced the local area over a few centuries just preceding the birth of Christ, and during this time they managed to take control of a significantly large area of northern Europe. They also reached the area where today lies Bratislava, settling down and forming a seat of considerable size here. Bratislava thus nowadays belongs to the oldest towns in Europe. The city also bears wit-

Important milestones of the city's history

1291 – Bratislava became a free royal town
1387 – Sigmund Luxemburg, who loved Bratislava, became Hungarian King
1430 – Bratislava was granted the privilege to mint coins
1436 – Bratislava was granted the privilege to use coat of arms
1458 – Matthias Corvinius ascended the Hungarian throne

1464 – Bratislava was confirmed to have a privileged status when King Matthias issued the Golden Bull
1468 – the existing privileges were extended by the right of the sword
1536 – Bratislava was promoted to the capital of the Hungarian Empire
1741 – Empress Maria Theresé was crowned in the city
1805 – Peace Treaty of Pressburg was signed in Bratislava
1840 – horse-driven railway was opened in the city
1919 – Pressburg changed name to Bratislava
1939 – Bratislava became the capital of independent Slovakia (so-called Slovak war-state)
1945 – the city was liberated (end of WWII)
1993 – Bratislava became the capital of modern independent Slovak state

Famous personalities

Matej Bel (1684 – 1749), polymath
Ján Andrej Segner (1704 – 1777), physicist, inventor
Ján Ctibor Fichtel (1732 – 1792), geologist
Wolfgang Kempelen (1734 – 1804), constructor
Chatam Sófer (1762 – 1839), rabbi, writer
Štefan Ladislav Endlich (1804 – 1849), botanist
Filip Lenard (1862 – 1947), physicist (1905 Nobel Prize winner)
Gustáv Malý (1879 – 1952), painter
Ladislav Dérer (1887 – 1960), doctor
Janko Alexy (1894 – 1970), painter
Daniel Rappant (1897 – 1988), historian
Ján Smrek (1898 – 1982), poet
Emil Belluš (1899 – 1979), architect

Hana Meličková (1900 – 1978), actress
Emil Boleslav Lukáč (1900 – 1979), poet
Ladislav Novomeský (1904 – 1976), poet, politician
Milo Urban (1904 – 1982), writer
Dezider Milly (1906 – 1971), painter
Alexander Moyzes (1906 – 1984), composer
Dionýz Ilkovič (1907 – 1980), physicist
Ján Kostra (1910 – 1975), poet
Alexander Matuška (1910 – 1975), literary scientist
Štefan Luby (1910 – 1976), lawyer, law professor
Jozef Budský (1911 – 1989), actor, director
Ján Cikker (1911 – 1989), composer
Rudolf Pribiš (1913 – 1984), sculptor
Dominik Tatarka (1913 – 1989), writer

Gustáv Husák (1913 – 1991), politician
Vladimír Bahna (1914 – 1977), director
Dezider Kardoš (1914 – 1991), music composer
Martin Kusý (1916 – 1989), architect
Bartolomej Urbanec (1918 – 1983), composer
Mikuláš Huba (1919 – 1986), actor
Ctibor Filčík (1920 – 1986), actor
Ľubomír Kellemberger (1921 – 1971), graphic artist
Andrej Lettrich (1922 – 1993), director
Vladimír Mináč (1922 – 1996), writer
Aladár Móži (1923 – 1983), violinist
Emil Mazúr (1925 – 1990), geographer
Miroslav Válek (1927 – 1991), poet, politician
Štefan Uher (1930 – 1993), actor

LEFT PAGE

▲ Plaque with an incomplete list of 11 kings and 8 queens crowned in the St. Martin's Cathedral
▼ The Main (Hlavné) Square in the historical centre of Bratislava

RIGHT PAGE

▲ Slovak Parliament building, Bratislava Castle, and St. Martin's Cathedral
◄ Primaciálny Palace is a highlight of Bratislava as well as the whole of Slovakia.
► Hummel Museum

ness to having been populated by Dacians, Germans, Romans and later also Avars and Slavs. Predecessors of today's Bratislavians settled here in the course of the 5th and the 6th centuries, forming a group of tribal principalities. Their fortified settlements in Bratislava and Devín even became important centres of the Great Moravia Empire. That's where the history of Bratislava begins to be recorded.

Bratislava Castle, a picturesque site nestled on a hillock, used to be a seat of the first Hungarian King Stephen I for a certain period – and from here he ruled over the empire. King Sigmund Luxemburg, the longest ruling king in the history of the Hungarian Empire (50 years), had an exceptionally warm relation to Bratislava, too. He granted Bratislava with the privilege to mint coins in its own mint. Fondness of Bratislava was also expressed by King Matthias Corvinius, who extended Bratislava's privileges with *jus gladii* ('right of the sword', meaning the right to carry out public executions). It was during Matthias's era that Bratislava's univer-

sity known as Academia Istropolitana was founded – using the oldest university in Europe (Bologna) as its prototype. In those days, Bratislava already ranked among the richest Hungarian towns.

Following the Hungarian defeat in the Battle of Moháč (1526), Bratislava was elevated to become Hungary's capital, which lasted until the Hungarian Empire managed to cast off Turkish supremacy. Being Hungary's capital meant being seat of the Council (parliament), the Hungarian Royal Chamber and the Council of Governors. Also, central state and clerical institutions moved from Budin to Bratislava, as well as the royal treasure and other valuables were brought here. The city was getting richer and more powerful, resisting all threats. Turks were ravaging the surroundings of Bratislava, but never entered the city itself. Indeed, it was a royal city – by 1830, coronations of Hungarian kings and queens were taking place here, including Empress Maria Therese – during a 40-year rule in which Bratislava flourished. The empress fell in love with the city as early as her cor-

LEFT PAGE
◀ St. Martin's Cathedral hosted coronations from 1563 – 1830.
▶ The golden crown on the tower of St. Martin's Cathedral

RIGHT PAGE
▲ Michalská Street and a well-known symbol of the city – Michael's Gate
▼ One of Bratislava's precious tapestries, dated 17th century

onation ceremony (taking place on June 25, 1741); later she frequented it, usually accompanied by ambitious aristocrats who often decided to build their mansion houses here eventually, in order to keep in close touch with the monarch. Bratislava started to grow remarkably, along with gradually gaining a respectable reputation. Maria Theresé had Bratislava Castle rebuilt, which lost its traditional function as a fortress and turned into a representative site. The city was lucky not to have experienced wars and other conflicts. This enabled crafts and trades to develop, as well as education, arts, spiritual life and culture. Bratislava was larger than Budapest and Budin (both in today's Hungary), and became an important centre of Europe not only politically, but also culturally. The 'city boom' was slowed down only by the Napoleonic Wars. Following the Battle of Austerlitz ('the battle of three emperors') in Moravia (the Czech Republic), a peace treaty confirming Napoleon's victory was signed in Bratislava. This happened on December 25, 1805.

Today, Bratislava is the most visited place in Slovakia, especially thanks to the great number of significant historical and cultural sights that it has in offer. The highlight among them is definitely Bratislava Castle, which has always been a symbol of the city. This quintessential part of Slovakia's capital catches one's eyes from quite a distance thanks to its size and characteristic look of a huge table turned upside down, resembling the castle in Toledo, Spain. Another Bratislava sight of national importance is St. Martin's Cathedral – the biggest temple church built in Gothic style that served as the coronation church between 1563 and 1830. Michael's Gate also unthinkably belongs to Bratislava's top sights – it's the last of formerly four gates through which the fortified medieval town used to be entered. Speaking of Bratislava's symbols in the downtown, we shouldn't omit Grassalkovich's Palace with its French-styled Garden, is now the seat of Slovak president and is thus known today as 'Presidential Palace'. This most beautiful example of gar-

den palaces in Bratislava was built in 1760 as a luxurious residence of Anton Grassalkovich, one of the most important representatives of the then Hungary. In Bratislava's Old Town, the building of Town Hall catches our eyes immediately. It's better known as the Old Town Hall, and dates back to the 15th century. Primaciálny Palace, a real jewel of Classicist palace architecture, stands in the vicinity of the Town Hall on Primaciálne Square. This monumental and luxurious palace was built in Classicist spirit (between 1778 and 1781) as a residence of Esztergom bishopric for the head of the Catholic Church in Hungary, Cardinal József Batthyányi. The most famous room in the palace is the Mirror Hall, which has witnessed the signing of documents of European importance. It is mentioned in French history books as the place where the aforementioned 1805 signing of the Peace Treaty of Pressburg took place. During restoration works on the palace, which was bought by the town in order to enlarge the Town Hall, a series of valuable tapestries were found inside its walls in 1903. Previous owner of the palace (the Esztergom archbishop) relinquished the tapestries, provided that they would be exposed. Since then, visitors to the palace have been able to see these extraordinarily valuable art pieces. The tapestries, woven between 1619 and 1688 in the royal weaving mill in the town of Mortlake, England, are made of wool and silk.

Postcards from Bratislava often feature another sight of the city – Good Shep-

herd's House, a splendid burgher house from the 18th century, considered to be one of the most beautiful houses in Bratislava, which houses a unique exposition of historical clocks installed here in 1975. An impressive sight in the city is also Church of St. Elisabeth of Hungary, which is thanks to its mostly blue decorations better known as the Blue Church. Speaking of churches, the Big Evangelical Church has great acoustics, so classical music concerts are often held here, while the Small Evangelical Church was erected in the place of former articulated wooden church from 1682, which was later dismounted. In the 1970s, the Small Church underwent a total restoration. Both these late-Baroque churches are typical for being built without presbyteries and towers. Evangelical lyceum, built nearby in Classicist style, was an important centre of Slovak national liberation struggle in the 19th century. Many Slovak awakeners studied and worked here, including Ľudovít Štúr, the man who codified standard Slovak. The lyceum building has survived to date, and today it's on the list of national cultural monuments. Evangelical worshippers originally had their church near the Old Town Hall, but was taken away from them in 1672, passing it under the administration by Jesuits, who made it consecrated to the Holiest Saviour. This all happened during the rule of King Leopold I, when re-Catholisation pressure was on the rise. Jesuits enriched the church's interior with sumptuous late-Baroque furnishings; however, the façade of the building remained plain, without decorations. The church offers one of the most beautiful Rococo pulpits in Slovakia. When you walk out from the church, you're standing on Franciscan Square, where you can admire the Column

LEFT PAGE
Monumental Bratislava Castle and its surroundings

RIGHT PAGE
◀ Devín Castle standing on a massive hill overlooking the confluence of the Danube and the Morava.

▶ Devín is a nice place to visit for people from all over.

of Virgin Mary the Victorious. Its exceptionality lies in the fact that it's the oldest of its kind in what was once the Hungarian Empire, belonging to a group of so-called 'victorious Marian columns' built by the Hapsburgs in observance of their military victories. On the other end of the square stands Franciscan Church, the oldest sacral building in Bratislava surviving to date. It is most likely to have been built by Hungarian King Ladislav IV, in order to mark his victory over Czech King Premysl Otokar II. The church is also known for the fact that newly crowned (in Bratislava) kings used to bestow a knighthood on selected noblemen. Opposite the church stands a Rococo palace from 1768, which gained its name after its last owner, Count Emil Mirbach. By his own request, Bratislava's municipal gallery is now seated here.

One of the oldest streets in Bratislava is Kapitulská Street, which was the main street of the town in the Romanesque period. As it was situated near St. Martin's Cathedral, mainly ecclesiastical dignitaries lived here, where they were moved from the castle, based on a Papal order in the early 13th century. The most sumptuous of these houses is the late-Renaissance two-storey Prepoštský (Provost's) Palace. The front yard of the palace has a sculpture featuring St. Elisabeth the Hungarian, who was born in Bratislava Castle in 1207. Nowadays the palace houses a seminary. The only secular palace-like building on Kapitulská Street was Esterházy's Palace, known for having surpassed the construction boom in the city for nearly a century. Originally, it belonged to the family of Listhys but was later bought by the Esterházys, whose name it received eventually.

Bratislava is sometimes referred to as the city of music and theatre. If you visit Bratislava in the autumn, you can take in classical music concerts held as part of Bratislavské hudobné slávnosti. World-class festival performances annually take place in the Reduta building and the nearby Opera House of the Slovak National Theatre.

BECKOV

The Impenetrable Castle

Forts and castles represent a rich vein for various folk tales. Their walls used to hide, and some of them still do, a number of unexplained mysteries, stories, legends, fairytales and rumours. So it is with the Beckov Castle – since time immemorial it has been steeped with thrilling and mysterious stories, largely because it stands on a precipitous rocky cliff that demands respect, and bodes something dangerous.

Beckov, once a small town, nowadays only a village, lies in a headland of a low-lying area near the Váh River, blessed with fertile soil that created favourable conditions for the population to flourish. Two individual settlements existed beneath the castle. The settlement, from which today's Beckov was formed, was seated directly under the castle. Its heyday began only when Emperor Sigmund gave the (originally royal) castle to Prince Stibor. The castle's domain included another ten villages, and what is now the town of Nové Mesto nad Váhom.

Both the village and its name are interesting. The first written record of the village traces back to 1352, but there's no doubt that Beckov already existed in the 13th century. Later references to it include the following names: Galaucz sive Beczkow, Bolunduz, Beczkow, Beczkoo, Beczkó, Beczko, and Becko. Who knows what's really true about the legend that the small town was given its name after a clown called Beck, for whom Prince Stibor had the castle built?

It is historically acknowledged, however, that King Sigmund Luxemburg granted Beckov town privileges in late 14th century (1392). Being one of very few smaller towns, Beckov was walled to such an extent that it basically shaped the forefront of the castle. The town in 1520 was granted the right to hold an annual market. Written records have it that wooden manor houses with courts used to be built in Beckov in those times, as only later were the houses made of bricks. The second oldest building around Beckov Castle, with the exception of the town walls, is the regional orphanage. Amber Manor, one of the local manor houses, includes an exposition documenting the history of the castle, the town (now village) and its famous natives, as well as traditional local crafts and historical furniture.

Beckov also offers quite a number of sacred sights, including Church of St. Stephen the King (built in 1424), Baroque-styled Franciscan Monastery and Church of St. Joseph the Foster Father (from between 1690 and 1692), Evangelical church (built in 1792), Classicist manor house, Jewish cemetery and Trinity Column. In the centre of Beckov, you can admire a remarkable linden park, with linden tress more than 150 years old.

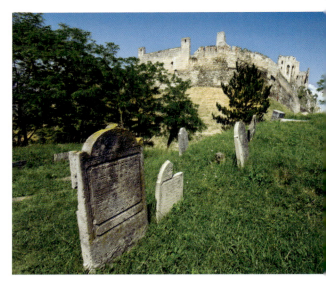

▲ Beckov Castle stands upon a steep 50-metre high outcrop.
▶ In 1729 the castle burnt out and went to ruins.
◀ The valley along the Váh offers good conditions for population.
▼ It became the property of Matúš Čák in late 13th century.

Important milestones in the village's history
1208 – the oldest written document of Beckov Castle
1352 – the record of local vicarage
1388 – the village was mentioned in another document, being referred to as 'Galaucz sive Beczkow'
1392 – Beckov was granted town privileges

1520 – Beckov was granted a privilege to hold its annual market

Famous personalities
Jozef Miloslav Hurban (1817 – 1888), politician, writer
Ján Ambro (1827 – 1890), doctor
Dionýz Štúr (1827 – 1893), writer
Ladislav Mednyánszky (1852 – 1919), painter

Places and sights worth visiting
Beckov Castle
Church of St. Stephen the King
Classicist manor house
Evangelical church

BOJNICE

Fairytale Beauty

Not only people and towns have their histories, trees do, too. Perhaps the best known tree in Slovakia is King Matthias's Linden in the small town of Bojnice. Legend has it that the tree was planted by one of Bojnice Castle's owners, Matúš Čák of Trenčín, in 1301. The linden has grown to become a majestic tree, which inherently belongs to the castle park in Bojnice as well as to this romantic town itself. Over the past centuries, the linden has witnessed many important historical events. King Matthias Corvinius used to hold sessions under the tree, from where he dictated many administrative decrees to be recorded. The first sentence of the documents usually began: *Sub nostris dilectis tillis Bojniciensibus (*Under our beloved linden of Bojnice).

However, Bojnice started to write down its history much earlier than the period when Matthias' documents were written. Archaeological findings have proven that the first people settled here almost a hundred thousand years ago.

A document issued by King Koloman in 1113 mentions another unique aspect of Bojnice – the thermal spa. It reads that the local hot springs were used for curative purposes even in those days. The spa resort was developing along with Bojnice Castle, with their mutual prosperity largely beholden to who owned the castle. Alexander Thurzo had the spa area built in the first half of the 16th century, and documents dating back to 1549 read that the area included water tanks with their contents at various temperatures. Another owner of the spa was Pavol Pálffy; and during his era the resort consisted of five pools under the same roof. The best pool was chiselled out from stone, while the others from wood. Its modern look was given to the spa area in 1930s by Ján Baťa, a famous owner of a family shoemaking corporation. Nowadays, the harmonious environment of the thermal springs and magnificent sceneries around are sought-after by many visitors, who make use of curative effects of the water coming out

from nine springs, especially to heal locomotive disorders.

The biggest attraction in Bojnice is the castle, however. It's one of the most beautiful and romantic castles in the whole country, steeped in many mysteries and hidden secrets. Actually, it used to be a royal castle before, but became the property of Matúš Čák of Trenčín at the end of the 13th century, as did the majority of castles in this region. Following his death, the castle had many different owners.

The greatest changes in the look of the castle were carried out during the 16th century, over the period of the Thurzos, but the look that the castle has now has been influenced mainly by the Pálffys, particularly Count Ján Pálffy. He called a Bratislava-based architect Jozef Hubert to rebuild the castle. Hubert had been looking for inspiration in the works of French architect Viollet le Duc, and managed to create an impressive look based on this. That's why the castle resembles French Romantic chateaux that can be seen in the valleys along the Loire River.

Count Ján Pálffy was fond of arts, and was a passionate collector of antiquities, which was reflected in the castle's furnishings. The Bojnice Altar now belongs to the most interesting works of art he collected. The altar is thought to be the work by Italian painter Nord di Cione, and dates as far back as the mid-14th century.

Thanks to Count Pálffy, Bojnice Castle turned into a fairytale-like site, but he didn't live long enough to view the ultimate result of the restoration works, as he died on June 2, 1908. His last wish was that all his palaces, chateaux and castles be open to the public. In Bojnice, his wish has come true – the castle's calendar is filled with public events all year round. The biggest annual event is the International Festival of Ghosts and Spirits, and tourists also like to visit the oldest ZOO in Slovakia situated right next to Bojnice castle.

▲ Bojnice Castle ranks among the loveliest cultural-historical sights in Slovakia.

▶ Bojnice altar, made by Italian Master n. di Cione Ortagno, dates back to the mid-14th century

▼ Hot-springs in Bojnice were known for their healing effects even in medieval times.

Important milestones in the town's history
1113 – the first record of Bojnice's hot springs
1299 – 1321 Bojnice settlement and the local castle were in possession of Matúš Čák of Trenčín

1527 – the Thurzos had the castle's core rebuilt between 1530 and 1599 – Bojnice was being constantly ravaged by Turks
1662 – Chapel of Ján Nepomucký was built in Bojnice
1663 – town walls were finished
1852 – the castle became the property of Ján Pálffy
1955 – ZOO was founded
1988 – major reconstruction of the castle began

Famous personalities
Ján Pálffy (1663 – 1751), Duke
Ján Pálffy (1829 – 1908), owner of the castle

Places and sights worth visiting
Bojnice Castle
Chapel of Ján Nepomucký
Spa resort
St. Martin's Church
ZOO

DUNAJSKÁ STREDA

The Centre of Žitný Island

It was probably King Belo III who founded a marketplace that later became the small town of Dunajská Streda, but the area had first been populated long before that time. Many archaeological findings bear witness to this, especially a burial place dating back to late Bronze Age, a mass finding of bronze objects representing Danubian tumular culture, the Roman-Barbarian settlement and a burial place from the times of the Great Moravia Empire.

Similar to other towns in the south of Slovakia, Dunajská Streda often used to change its name in the past. According to written documents available, it used to be called Svridahel, Zeredahel, Zredhel, Szerdahely, Serdahely, in early 20th century Dunaszerdahely, and after 1948 Dunajská Streda (which, in Slovak, literally means 'Danubian Wednesday'). The name was given to the town according to the fact that markets were held here every Wednesday.

The town's history is also interesting, changing throughout the past according to who was the ruler. As a village, Dunajská Streda was the property of the Esztergom archbishopric. Later, based on a decree issued by King Sigmund Luxemburg in 1405, it became a serf town. Between 1600 and 1848, the town was owned by the Pálffys, having status of a town under control of local squire, and was granted a privilege to hold markets and fairs. Dunajská Streda was then well known for grain and cattle fairs. Later, a number of craftsmen settled here, including shoemakers, hatters and coopers, which made the town a famous centre of crafts and trade in Žitný Island.

Famous personalities
Anna Minichová (1924 – 1988), writer

Places and sights worth visiting
Art-MA Gallery (private)
Church of the Assumption
Evangelical church
Gallery of Contemporary Hungarian Artists
Museum of Žitný Island
Thermal pool

Important milestones in the town's history
1162 – the oldest record of the town
1405 – Dunajská Streda became a serf town
1574 – Dunajská Streda was granted town privileges
1895 – railway was built, linking the town with Bratislava

Dunajská Streda's sacral buildings and cultural monuments best illustrate its prosperity. The most valuable sacral sight here is the Roman Catholic Church of the Assumption, originally a Gothic building from the 14th century. Since then it has undergone a number of restorations and facelifts, but precious original wall paintings in the presbytery and on the southern façade remain. In the medieval times, a market square was formed around the church, and today it actually represents the core of the town. Evangelical church, built in neo-Gothic style in 1883, is also worth checking out. In the first half of the 18th century, the Baroque-styled Yellow Chateau was built under the direction of bishop Mikuláš Kondé.

The building today houses the Museum of Žitný Island, which includes a permanent ethnographical and archaeological exposition. You can also visit exhibitions by the Slovak National Gallery, installed in the so-called Vermes Villa, built in historicist style at the turn of the 19th and the 20th century. Graphic artists and painters have the opportunity to present their works in the Gallery of Contemporary Hungarian Artists, and those of Hungarian origin in the Art-MA Gallery. In the place where Jewish synagogue used to stand, you can see a new memorial (called 'Memento') which commemorates the deportations of more than three thousand Jews from Dunajská Streda during WWII.

LEFT PAGE

▲ Vermes Villa houses expositions run by the Slovak National Gallery.

◄ Yellow Chateau is the seat of Žitnoostrovné Museum.

▼ Church of the Assumption is the most precious sacral sight in the town.

RIGHT PAGE

Billabong of the Danube is one of natural highlights

KOMÁRNO

The Town with the Square of Europe

Areas along the basins of the two biggest rivers in Slovakia – the Váh and the Danube – have always enjoyed rulers' interests, thanks to being the most advantageous places strategically. Rulers used to build massive defence systems along the rivers, convinced that it's water that can keep them away and make them safe from their enemies. It was perhaps Romans who were the first to build a fortress upon the Danube. They were followed by others, including Slavs and old Hungarians. Historians say this is implied based on archaeological findings, but the oldest details on a fortress building date back only to the period of King Belo IV. However, an anonymous document reads that a town was founded around the castle

called Komárom. Even earlier, three market settlements emerged here: 'villa Camarum', 'villa Kezw' and 'villa St. Androe'. Komárno as such is for the first time mentioned in historical documents dated 1037. It received town privileges from King Belo IV in 1265.

In medieval times, the town was in bloom, and became a popular place for meetings of many rulers. Prosperous Komárno was a place which even King Matthias Corvinius used to frequent for rest and pleasure. Corvinius had his own castle built here, which (in terms of defence) was of great importance to the whole country in the 16th century, especially in the times of Turkish expansion. During the rule of King Ferdinand I, the medieval castle was rebuilt into a well-

▲ Municipal coat of arms

◄ ► Unique 'Square of Europe' in Komárno

▼ Neo-Renaissance building of the Town Hall

Important milestones in the town's history
1331 – Komárno was promoted from village to town
1663 – construction works on the fortress began, based on the command by King Leopold I

1745 – Komárno was granted free royal town privileges
1763, 1765, 1783 – earthquakes

Famous personalities
Mór Jókai (1825 – 1904), writer
Franz Lehár (1870 – 1948), music composer

Places and sights worth visiting
Calvinist church
Church of Orthodox Serbian Confession

Komárno's fortress
Military church
Podunajské Museum
Square of Europe
St. Andrew's Church
St. Joseph's Chapel
St. Rozalia's Church
Town Hall
Zichy Palace

defended fortification. Italian architects were invited, in order to build a perfect site -technically securing it to unconquerable. That's how the fortress became the greatest bastion fortification in central Europe. More than a century later, the fortress was extended, annexing a new site, pentagon-shaped and with stellar-vaulted walls. A bridge built over a moat connected both fortifications. The whole fortress was indeed unconquerable, and resisted all Turkish invasions. But even if having impenetrable sites, man is helpless against massive natural disasters. This was proven to be true even here in 1763, when the fortress was destroyed by a strong earthquake.

In the course of the 18th century, Komárno, thanks to its advantageous location on the junction of water and earthbound roads, became one of the most important towns in the country, flourishing with crafts and trade. In view of this boom, Empress Maria Therese granted it with free royal town privileges in 1745. Following another earthquake several years later, Emperor Joseph II disbanded the imperial army representatives previously located here, and donated the local royal lands to the town. The defence system revived only when Napoleon's army posed a military threat. Then, Emperor Ferdinand I decided that Komárno would become the strongest fortress in the monarchy. The new system of fortification (built in 1809) with two gates was connected with the fortress itself and encircled the whole

town. The remains of the fortification system are now a historical monument of European importance, as well as a national cultural monument.

In the past, Komárno became famous for shipbuilding industry, and local dockyards are the biggest manufacturers of riverboats and sea-ships in central Europe even today. The port in Komárno belongs to the largest ones on the Danube.

The town has several historical sights, too – all of them documenting cultural and social developments of Komárno. The dominant sight is Zichy Palace, which dates back to the 17th century, but remarkable is also the neo-Renaissance Town Hall building. The catastrophes that hit the town in the past largely influenced local sacral buildings, from which only the following have survived: St. Andrew's Church, St. Rozalia's Church, Calvinist church and a military church. The latter was formerly a Franciscan church with a monastery. The diversity of religious confessions is proven by the existence of the Calvinist church and Church of Orthodox Serbian Confession, in the interior of which you can admire a collection of Orthodox icons from the 17th and the 18th century.

Komárno is also very proud of its Square of Europe – a unique construction work designed by local architects. Buildings here, all in styled form, represent historical architecture typical for individual European countries.

▲ Fortress in Komárno used to be the largest bastion fortification in central Europe.

▼ 'Square of Europe'

LEVICE

The Ghost Crying at the Castle Walls

The dominant site in the town of Levice, nestled in the east of Podunajská Lowland - where the lowland meets the foothills of Štiavnické Mountains, is Levice Castle.

Just like many other Slovak castles and forts, the castle here used to belong to Matúš Čák of Trenčín for a certain period. His rule appears to have been very popular, because the legend of Levice Castle has it that after his death a member of his crew was planning to assassinate Matúš's successor, King Charles Robert.

The murder plans didn't work out and the king thus commanded that his innocent family be murdered in return. It's said that his beautiful daughter was killed at the castle's walls. Since then, legend has it that her crying ghost appears here every night, roaming near the walls, seeking her husband and children. Only when the dawn comes and the night fades does the ghost disappear.

This is the legend, but the facts concerning the castle say that it was built in the 13th century. Following the death of Matúš Čák, it became a royal property.

Castles have always been attractive to people, who usually move to be as close to

them as possible in order to at least find some jobs and the security that such a battlement offers.

This is exactly the case of Levice Castle during the 14th century - people from surrounding villages began moving in to form a village called Nové Levice (New Levice), also known as Veľké Levice (Great Levice).

In those days the castle was an important, respected and serious seat, because King Louis I the Great used to call palatine sessions here. However, in later times the castle was an item to be donated: in 1388, King Sigmund Luxemburg gave it (including the surrounding lands) to a feudal lord Ladislav of Šarovce, whose son Peter decided to be called Lévai of Levice. They owned the castle for approximately the next 150 years, then it became a royal property again.

Anyway, the castle's blaze of glory was still to come. This came during the Turkish invasions, when Turks captured the area spreading southwards of Levice. In 1664, Turks suffered serious losses at a battle that went down in history as 'the great battle of Levice'.

◄ Levice Castle, dated late 13th century

► Tekovské Museum houses historical collections from all around the region.

▼ Ceramics of Tekov (museum's collection)

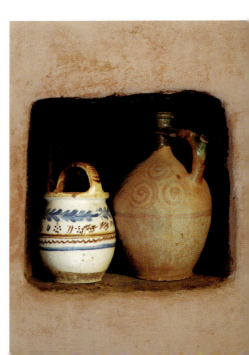

Important milestones in the town's history
1156 - the first written record of Levice
1318 - the record of Levice Castle

1388 - Levice was granted privileges concerning holding markets and collecting tolls
1614 - Staré (Old) Levice and Nové (New) Levice merged to form a single town

Famous personalities
Anton Celestin Radványi (1911 - 1978), writer

Places and sights worth visiting
Burgher houses on the square
Calvinist church
Chateau in the village of Kalinčiakovo
Dobó Chateau
Evangelical church
Jewish synagogue
Levice Castle
Romanesque chapel
St. Joseph's Church
St. Michael's Church
Tekovské Museum
Town Hall

The castle was perhaps most seriously destroyed in 1709 by Rákóczi's rebel army, and later was used only as a storehouse.

Nowadays, the castle area is administrated by the Tekovské Museum, where you can see a number of interesting exhibits, including the African collection of Koloman Kittenberger, Levice's famous native globetrotter.

The history of Levice is closely connected to the history of Levice Castle – even the first written record of the town (from 1318) mentions the existence of the castle. The settlement round the castle (i.e. Nové, or Veľké Levice) was mentioned only later. The settlement area, however, was granted the right to hold markets and collect tolls already in 1388. The people of Levice were only worried of Turks and their raids, the result of which was the town being burnt out several times.

István Dobó became the owner of Levice and captain of the castle in 1558. He annexed a Renaissance-Baroque walled manor house to the castle that is today known as Dobó Chateau.

The heyday period in the town was the 17th century, when it became the centre of the Tekov domain and a market town famous for its local crafts.

Levice is rich in both secular and sacral sights, the most impressive of which are St. Michael's Church and St. Joseph's Church (the latter was built in Baroque style and formerly was a Franciscan monastery).

Levice has always been a town of several religious confessions, and that's why you can find here also Evangelical and Calvinist churches, as well as a Jewish synagogue.

The oldest sacral sight, and architectonically highly valuable, is a Romanesque chapel which dates back to the 12th century.

Interesting enough is also the building of Town Hall and several burgher houses. We shouldn't omit traditional 'secular' opportunities in Levice, such as well-known Levice fairs, so-called Castle Games, and bathing in thermal waters in the spa resort called 'Margita a Ilona'.

To mark the 850th anniversary of the first record of the town of Levice, the town organised a so-called Maxi Goulash party in 2006. More than 7,000 people were able to partake, helping put the event into the Guinness Book of Records as the largest event of its kind.

▲ Folk architecture – reservation in the village of Brhlovce

▼ Exposition of folk dwellings

MALACKY

A Stopping Point on the European Postal Route

Our visit to another Slovak town begins a bit unusually – in crypts hidden under the local church and monastery.

In the town of Malacky, underneath the Monastery and Church of the Immaculate, more specifically underneath its St. Ann's Chapel, there are crypts containing the remains of nearly 200 people. Franciscan monks built the church and its underground intending to use the space beneath the ground to bury members of their order, following the dictates of their ancient cult. These crypts also contain dead bodies of several of the last Pálffys, whose family line was very widespread, owning manors all around Slovakia as well as abroad. As they owned a lot of properties and lands around here, they eventually decided to be buried in Malacky. In St. Ann's Chapel, which was originally a house of worship containing an altar, they had holes hollowed out in walls where coffins could be slipped inside. The coffins are covered by marble plates and engraved with gold inscription. The silver cassette showcased in a special separated vitrine contains the heart of John Pálffy. Originally, the heart of his father Paul (said to have had miraculous powers) was kept here, too. The legends have it that before any of the wars in the past, the heart was bleeding, as if crying. Anyway, during the WWI, the legendary heart got lost.

Among other attractions of the church is the Holy Staircase, which is a masterful copy of the stairs that Jesus Christ had to walk on his ultimate journey. Similar copies of the staircase are only seen in the Vatican and Jerusalem. To walk it, you have to enter from the left side – on bended knee. That's because, legend has it, beneath each of the steps there is the body of a saint immured.

All these unusual things only prove that Malacky has an interesting history. The town was developing according to the rulers of the past, and Malacky grew and flourished not only economically, but also socially, culturally and spiritually.

Important milestones in the town's history

1206 – the first written record of the area of today's Malacky
1231 – Hungarian King Andrew II divided the land here among his loyal war allies
1771 – Malacky joined the state postal service route
1573 – Malacky was granted a set of privileges to hold markets
1577 – the town's coat of arms was created
1885 – Malacky became a district town
1891 – railroad was built to cross the town

Famous personalities

Martin Benka (1888 – 1971), painter
Ľudo Zúbek (1907 – 1969), writer
Vlado Müller (1936 – 1996), actor

Places and sights worth visiting

Church of the Immaculate Conception
Church of the Holy Trinity

LEFT PAGE
▲ Franciscan Church of the Immaculate Conception
◄ Holy Staircase in the Church of the Immaculate Conception
▶ Originally a Rennaissance work, the chateau in Malacky was a sumptuous aristocratic seat in the early 19th century.

RIGHT PAGE
▲ Crypt beneath the Church of the Immaculate Conception
◄ Synagogue in the centre of town
▼ The Habani site in Velké Leváre represents, to date, the largest original Habani dwelling in Europe.

If we wish to trace back to the oldest documented history of the town, we need to go back to 1206, when Hungarian King Andrew II began to divide the uninhabited lands to his loyal 'magnificios', who had previously lent him a helping hand in wars he led. In this border region (near the frontiers with Bohemian lands, today the Czech Republic), there was a small settlement along the so-called Malinský stream, which later started to be called Malaczka – which later changed to today's name Malacky. It was feudal lords the Hont-Poznans (in Hungarian history known as 'the counts from Svätý Jur and Pezinok') who eventually owned the whole settlement. On their properties here they built Plavecký Castle for the king, which they later received (in return) as their own property. Later in the course of history, the domain together with the castle was pawned to several feudal lords and noble families, the best known of which was perhaps the Balašš family. The Balaššs decided to make Malacky the seat of their domain. Amid the local swamps and hunting grounds, they had a hunting lodge built, introduced Evangelical Confession among the locals, built a presbytery, and founded the first school here.

The family died off in the 17th century, and the whole domain was sold to the Pálffys, who owned it for the next three hundred years. Under their influence the confession of the faithful was changed in the town. They had the hunting lodge rebuilt into a monastery, and in 1652 they invited Franciscans here. The building of a large church – Church of the Holy Trinity – topped off the 're-Catholisation' of the domain. In the middle of the 17th century, the Pálffys built a grand manor house in Malacky. (Until recently it was used as the administrative seat for the local hospital).

The town was gradually growing and flourishing with a lively business spirit. In 1771, Malacky was annexed to the state postal service route and a post chaise office was established here as a stop on the route from Bratislava via Stupava, Malacky, Moravský Sv. Ján through Holíč. Holíč was a town right on the border with the Bohemian Kingdom, which meant a direct postal connection with Prague. Malacky was thus tied in with the European as well as the transatlantic postal networks.

Education facilities in Malacky are also worth mentioning, as it's always been on a very good level. Franciscans had their own secondary school built sometimes during the Enlightenment Era, while in 1889 Countess Margita built a school for girls in the town, which was quite extraordinary as only boys had been eligible to attend schools until then. In 1919 the town school was established in Malacky, and in 1927 the Franciscan grammar school was founded.

MODRA

The Town of Wine and Sun

The Small Carpathians usually connotes wine and sun, and so do the towns and villages lining the mountains from the eastern side. All of them are widely known for local viniculture and wine-related traditions, but it's not only wine that this region is famous for – the area has always been known for its rich cultural heritage and splendid nature.

The town of Modra lies the closest to the foothills of the Small Carpathians, and this is why the contact with nature is the most apparent here. The hills around are practically fully covered by cottages and tourist paths, very popular among both locals and citizens of Slovakia's capital Bratislava, which is not far from here. In the past, Modra was perhaps best known for being a workplace of Ľudovít Štúr, a national awakener and the most significant codifier of the standard Slovak language in the nation's history. Tourists walking from Modra to the Zochova Cottage often stop on the Zámčisko Hill, where the remains of a former Slavic fortified settlement can be seen. Not to be missed is Štúr's footbridge, which is at the place where Ľudovít Štúr used to like to go for walks when he lived in Modra.

Modra was once one of the towns associated in the West Slovak Pentapolitana – five vineyard towns, including also Bratislava, Trnava, Pezinok and Svätý Jur. In 1361, Modra was granted town privileges, however it remained a serf town. The town, just like many others in Slovakia, was always facing Hussite raids. Following one such attack in 1428, Modra was totally ravaged. Salvation for the town came when King Sigmund gave it to a feudal lord Michael Országh de Guth, whose descendants owned the town for more than 130 years. This was something of a golden era for the town, as it was economically flourishing and growing also in social terms – in 1569 it attained political sovereignty, while in 1607 it was promoted to a free royal town. One of the most important of the granted privileges guaranteed Modra the right to build walls, so the town walls were put up here. During the 17th century, the glory of the town vanished, following the series of

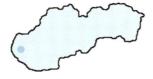

Important milestones in the town's history
1361 – Modra was granted town privileges
1437 – town was given to a feudal lord Michael Országh de Guth

1569 – Modra was promoted to a free town
1607 – Modra was promoted to a royal town
1702 – Imperial army set the town on fire
1705 – the town suffered from another destructive fire

Famous personalities
Ľudovít Štúr (1815 – 1856), writer, politician, linguist,
  national awakener
Ivan Branislav Zoch (1843 – 1921), compiler of encyclopaedias
Jozef Ilečko (1909 – 1986), painter
Rudolf Fábry (1915 – 1982), poet
Michal Rapoš (1925 – 1979), electric engineer

Places and sights worth visiting
Burgher houses on the square
Church of St. John the Baptist
Church of St. Stephen the King
Červený Kameň Castle
Evangelical churches
Gallery of Ignác Bizmayer
Memorial to Ľudovít Štúr
Museum of Ľudovít Štúr
Town walls

catastrophes – imperial soldiers set it on fire, and what wasn't burnt at that time was finished off during another extensive fire in 1705. Anyway, wine growing was always a good business, so the town recovered from the previous disasters quite rapidly. In addition, Modra had always been bustling with cultural and social life, attracting new people to settle here. Modra is also known for having been influenced by the massive wave of the Reformation Movement, which spread rapidly among the locals in the past. In 1714 and 1715, the Evangelical Confession built two churches here. These Protestants also supported education, which was at a good level in Modra. Successful development of the growing town was in 1729 marred by another fire, during which the churches, schools and ecclesiastical buildings were seriously damaged.

Wine growing brought the biggest fame to Modra, but also local crafts were widely known – especially potters and ceramics producers. In a rotund-like bastion from the 17th century, which used to be a part of the town walls, today we can find the unique Gallery of Ignác Bizmayer – famous master, producer of figural ceramics, whose works (figurines) feature the lives of folks, their customs and traditions.

Talking about and visiting Modra, we shouldn't miss out the best-preserved castle in the whole of Slovakia – Červený Kameň ('Red Rock') Castle, located in the vicini-

ty of the nearby village of Častá. This originally early-Gothic building, formerly called Bibersburg ('Beaver's Fort'), was built in the beginning of the 13th century, and for two centuries it was used as a royal defence castle for counts from nearby towns. In 1535 it was sold to the Fuggers, rich merchants from Augsburg who had a Renaissance-styled fortress built nearby. The fortress served as a stock for obtained goods. The corner citadels of the fortress were used as defence facilities, including enough space for eventual use of cannons. In 1588 the castle fell into the hands of Mikuláš (Nicholas) Pálffy, hereditary mayor of Bratislava. Following the series of necessary changes and restorations, the castle was gradually turned into a manor. Its painted decorations are mostly from this period, especially painted stucco decoration of the impressive hall – Salla Terena. Most of the castle's rooms are today used for repository purposes.

The Pálffys also built a chateau in the nearby village of Budmerice, now representing one of the very few Romantic buildings in Slovakia inspired by foreign architecture. Moreover, it's located in a large English park that gradually melds into a forest-park, creating an important part of the natural scenery of this representative seat. Today, Slovak and foreign men of literature usually meet in the chateau to take the advantage of its wonderful surroundings in order to garner inspiration for their artistic endeavours.

LEFT PAGE

▲ Memorial to Ľudovít Štúr on the square
◄ Červený Kameň Castle
▶ Rotund bastion used to be part of the town walls.

RIGHT PAGE

◄ Budmerice's lovely chateau is now the House of Slovak Writers.
▶ Renaissance altar in St. George's Church in Svätý Jur
▼ The Upper Gate also used to be part of the town walls.

27

NITRA

Mother of Slovak Towns

Out of all Slovak cities and towns, Nitra is the one likely to be the most imbued with legends. The area has always been particularly attractive, which can be proven through numerous archaeological findings from all stages of the Stone Age. It was Slavs who settled here already in the 5th and 6th centuries, causing Nitra to become a political, economic and cultural centre of the people living there a century later. At the turn of the 8th and 9th centuries, the famous and historically-important Nitra Principality was established here, headed by the even more famous Prince Pribina, the first ruler of so-called Sloviens, who are considered to be ancestors of the modern Slovaks. The fates and fortunes of past rulers were often up and down, and Pribina was driven away from Nitra to make way for Prince Rastislav to sit on the prince's throne. In 846, when Rastislav became the ruler over the Great Moravian Empire, his nephew Svätopluk took over the throne in Nitra. At that time the city was an impressive political, economic and cultural centre. Evidence to this is that Rastislav in 863 invited Byzantine Christian proselytisers Constantine and Methodius, who brought the translation of the Holy Writ into the Slavic language, and also laid the basics for the Slavic script.

Anyone who is the least bit interested in Slavic history recognises the name Svätopluk in connection with one of the best known Slovak legends – the legend of King Svatopluk's three rods. It's a parable that richly demonstrates the need for unity, because – as legend has it – a bundle of rods is harder to break than individual rods. Through this, Svätopluk wanted to emphasise that only unity and togetherness of his three sons will ensure invincibility for the brothers and wealth for the empire. However, Svätopluk's longing for unity didn't come true after his death in 894. His sons divided the Great Moravia among themselves, and the glorious story of the empire ended ingloriously. Raids by Hungarians and Bavarians in 906 killed Great Moravia for good.

Nitra managed to preserve its strategic importance throughout the next two centuries anyway. Only then the principality became part of the Hungarian Empire – when the Esztergom bishopric was established, the Nitra area was merged with it. Two precious written documents are preserved in the archives of the Nitra bishopry – the so-called Zobor Charter, the oldest known original writings in Slovak, which date back to 1111 and 1113. Since 1111, a Benedictine monastery of St. Hypolit has stood on Zobor Hill, and Nitra Castle was the seat of Arpadian dukes – Belo, Gejza and Lajos.

The next milestone in the city's history was September 2, 1248, when King Belo IV granted Nitra free royal town privileges. But the glory of being a free royal town didn't last for long, because the approaching war (involving moot borderlands between Bohemian and Hungarian kingdoms) prevented the town from flourishing. In 1288, the town of Nitra became the property of the Nitra bishopric, meaning that it turned into a bound serf town, usurped by powerful medieval ruler Matúš Čák until his death in 1321.

Important milestones in the city's history

828 – Prince Pribina had the first Christian church in what is now Slovakia built in Nitra
863 – Christian mission of Byzantine brothers Constantine and Methodius came, with the couple bringing a translation of the Holy Writ
894 – Svatopluk's sons divided the Great Moravia among themselves
1111 and 1113 – Zobor papers were written, the oldest known original writings in Slovak
1248 – Nitra was granted free royal town privileges
1288 – free royal town privileges scrapped
1440 – town captured by soldiers of Ján Jiskra of Brandýs
1663 – a year's occupation by Turks
1708 – Rákóczi's guerrillas capitulated in Nitra
1836 – printing plant established in Nitra
1987 – Upper Town area declared the town's historical preserve

Famous personalities

Ján Vavrincov of Račice (birth and death unknown), Hussite professor at Charles University in Prague
Janko Jesenský (1874 – 1945), poet, prose writer, translator
Július Bártfay (1888 – 1979), sculptor, painter, graphic artist and restorer
Štefan Krčméry (1892 – 1955), poet
Gejza Vámoš (1901 – 1956), author
Edmund Massányi (1907 – 1966), painter, restorer
Štefan Králik (1909 – 1983), playwright
Ján Pásztor (1912 – 1988), bishop
Pavol Strauss (1912 – 1994), author and humanist theorist
Dominik Tatarka (1913 – 1989), author
Janko Silan (1914 – 1984), poet
Rudolf Jašík (1919 – 1960), prose writer
Anna Martvoňová (1922 – 1990), opera singer
Ján Chryzostom Korec (1924), Cardinal
Ján Kákoš (1927 – 1996), playwright
Daniel Bidelnica (1957), painter

Places and sights worth visiting

Bishop's Palace
Bishop's Pálffy's Gate
Castle's well and plague column with statue of Immaculata
Church and the Franciscan monastery
Great Seminary
Kluch's Palace
Monastery with the Piarist church
Monastery with the Vincentian church
Nitra Castle
Regional administration office building
Small Seminary with a statue of Prince Pribina
St. Emeram's Church
St. Stephen's Church
Svorad Cave
Synagogue
Vazul Tower
Zobor Hill

LEFT PAGE
Nitra Castle is the city's dominant sight.

RIGHT PAGE
Interior of St. Emeram's Church

LEFT PAGE
▲ ▼ St. Emeram's Church and the Romanesque wall at Nitra Castle

RIGHT PAGE
St. Emeram's Church in detail

The coming centuries were trying for Nitra, as no war front missed the town, which, of course, had negative effects on its development. In 1440 the town was conquered by Jan Jiskra of Brandýs (nowadays the Czech Republic), and later by the Polish King Kazimir. In 1663 Nitra was taken over by Turks. The occupation lasted one year, and they burned down the town before they left. Another such disaster came later, when Rákóczi's (Hungarian) guerrillas stayed in Nitra for five years. When the consequent uprising was suppressed, the town was in ruins. Later, restorations and constructions of new buildings begun in 1710 and featured the Baroque spirit. Then, many architectonic highlights in the centre of the town emerged, both the castle and cathedral rebuilt, Church of Our Lady repaired and the Piarist building complex finished. In Upper Town (in Slovak: 'Horné mesto', which was then a name for part of the town) individual parts of Great Seminary and Small Seminary were built, plus a Franciscan church was restored. Also, a stone bridge at the entrance to the castle and a plague column are worth checking out. Early 19th century was featured by empiricist philosophy a Classicist style, in which the town's historical part was built. Nitra soon began prospering and regained its cultural wealth. Many great men of the

nation stayed here, and a printing plant was established in 1836. Other important sites, very sumptuous in style, built in the town at that time included the regional administration office building, followed by the Classicist building housing the theatre in 1882, plus several bourgeois residences. Nitra also experienced an extensive housing boom in the 1930s, after the regulation of the Nitra River was completed near the newly emerged area of Dolné mesto (Lower Town). Houses built here began to be liquidated after WWII however, as this part of the town had been damaged, and an extensive construction of blocks of flats later went up in their place.

The dominant feature of the city and its close surroundings, and the highlight of the sights here, is Nitra Castle, built in the 11th century on the grounds of its old precursor – a large Slavic fortified settlement. Favourite Nitra's landmarks for tourists also include Zobor Hill, famous for its Svorad Cave, which received its name after St. Svorad, who, a legend attributed to Maur has it, used to live here as a hermit in the 11th century. He was canonised in 1083 and is buried in the castle's cathedral. Speaking of sacral sites in Nitra, remarkable is also Calvary, which dates from the 19th century and consists of as many as 14 chapels (Stations of the Cross).

LEFT PAGE
▲ Late-Classicist building of Small Seminary, dated second half of the 19th century
▼ Wall painting on the ceiling inside St. Emeram's Church

RIGHT PAGE
Romanesque St. Michael's Church in Dražovce, dated early 12th century

NOVÉ ZÁMKY

Modern Renaissance Fortress

The bells were ringing all around Eu rope the day the Imperial army liber ated the town of Nové Zámky, follow ing a 22 year period of the town having been occupied by Turks - so significant was the event. This happened on August 19, 1685 - the date went down the his tory and is written in gold letters in the town's chronicle.

Nové Zámky emerged in the 16th cen tury, in the place of four former villages devastated by Turkish raids. Indeed, the town's history was connected with Turks from the beginning. The first mention of the town comes from 1545, when the anti Turkish fortification emerged here, being the first such fortress on the left bank of the Nitra River. Between 1576 and 1580, a large stone fortress was begun to be built on the other bank of the river, then rank ing among the latest fortification construc tions in Europe. The fortress was project ed by Italian architects Ottavio and Giulio Baldigari, and had a regular hexagon shaped ground plan with massive bas tions to be used for gunnery. Walls of the fortress were totally encircled by a wide moat, which was connected with the river, aimed to forestall Osman (Turkish) army approaching Vienna. When the construc

tion works were finished, Nové Zámky was considered to be one of the best built fortresses in the Austrian Hungarian Em pire. For a long time it was proved resist ant to the Turks, but was eventually con quered in 1663 by their army of around 200,000. The town began to suffer un der the rule of Turkish soldiers, whose in comes represented taxes and natural lev ies paid by serfs. The liberation of Nové Zámky in 1685 was redemption indeed for the local people.

The modern history of Nové Zámky started to be written in 1691, when Arch bishop Juraj Szécsényi issued a document granting it town privileges. The fortifica tion was now becoming pointless in the town, so King Charles III ordered it torn down, which took place between 1724 and 1726. The town began to prosper econom ically, providing a comfortable environ ment for craftsmen and tradesmen. Trains began to run through the town in 1850 on a railway route connecting Vienna - Brati slava - Budín, while in 1892 a long ferro concrete bridge over the Nitra River was built here.

In 1935, Nové Zámky citizens staged a big celebration of the 250th anniversa ry of the town's liberation, and unveiled

Important milestones in the town's history
1545 – the first written record of Nové Zámky
1663 – the fortress was conquered by the Turkish army
1685 – the town was liberated by the Imperial army

Famous personalities
Anton Bernolák (1762 – 1813), linguist
Jozef Ružička (1916 – 1989), linguist
Ernest Zmeták (1919 – 2004), painter

Places and sights worth visiting
Calvary
Church of the Saint Cross
Evangelical church
Franciscan church and monastery
Geographic Museum
Holy Trinity Chapel
Holy Trinity sculptural group
Lutheran church

LEFT PAGE
◄ Precious archaeologist site in the village of Bajč
► Baroque sculptural group of Holy Trinity

RIGHT PAGE
◄ Roman sarcophagus in St. James's Church in Želiezovce
► Church of the Saint Cross on the square
▼ Franciscan monastery

a monument which is now a significant cultural site.

The dominant sight in the town is a Roman-Catholic Church of the Saint Cross, built in 1584 and 1585. Since then, it underwent several restorations. This originally neo-Gothic building was completely burnt out in 1810, only part of it (including vestry and the presbytery's Eternal Light) survived. The building was substantially rebuilt in 1877, when the church took on a neo-Classicist character and look.

One of the most beautiful sites in the town – the Calvary, built in 1877, following the Baroque spirit – spreads out on the southern side of the former hexagon-shaped fortress area. Other sacral sights in Nové Zámky include the Evangelical, Lutheran and Franciscan churches, the latter of which features a monastery. In the early 18th century, the church was in the hands of František Rákóczi II and Mikuláš Bercsényi, who had the monastery section extended, respecting the

original architecture of the complex. Another renovation of the church took place in late 19th century. Down under the church, there used to be a crypt where representatives of the monastery and the town were buried. Their remains are kept in the crypt at the municipal cemetery nowadays. Today, the monastery is used partly as an exposition run by the municipal Požitavské Museum and partly as a lodging house for Franciscan clergy. Famous linguist and codifier of the first version of standard Slovak language (based on Western Slovak dialects) Anton Bernolák rests in peace in the Holy Trinity Chapel, which was built in Baroque style in the place of a former stone cemetery. He lived in the town for 16 years until his death in 1813.

The town is also proud of the Baroque sculptural group that features the Holy Trinity. This was installed to commemorate the plague epidemics that struck the town in 1740.

PEZINOK

A Short Stop on the Small Carpathian Wine Route

From Slovakia's capital, Bratislava, the roads break up to lead to almost all corners of the country and one of these roads takes us to the vineyards, wine bars, wine houses and wine cellars nestled in the Small Carpathians. It was thus given the name Small-Carpathian Wine Route. On the route, right next to Bratislava, sits the ancient small town of Svätý Jur, once a free royal town. It managed to keep its distinctive rural character until today. The core of the town, which is a preserved municipal sight, is formed by typical vintage houses with high gates, to make it easy for horse-driven cars carrying harvested grapes to pass and enter the backyard on their way to the cellars and winepress houses. The town is also known for St. George's Church, in the inside of which we have a chance to admire a rare early-Renaissance stone altar with the carving of St. George in the middle. The other churches in the town are: Church of the Holy Trinity and Evangelical church.

After the road from Bratislava cuts across the village of Limbach and we make it across a short flat land, we're entering the town of Pezinok right away.

It's obvious at first glance that Pezinok is a kingdom of vinedressers. However, on second glance, the town makes us feel surprised when it comes to a number of unusual buildings. Among the oldest ones is the local chateau – originally a fort built in the 13th century, which was later rebuilt in the Baroque spirit on the command of its then owners, the Pálffys. This resulted in the construction losing its fortress-like character. The inside of the chateau gives us a chance to admire a well-preserved majolica hearth, which has Italian origin. In the present, the chateau is used as a trendy wine restaurant. The dominant building of Pezinok's square is the Town Hall, which was erected around 1600 and later restored. Especially worth checking out on the square are two corner-rounded alcoves, oriented towards the square. The whole square in Pezinok is skirted by burgher hous-

es, which are built as typical vintage houses with footprints in the shape of the letter U, and represent a very characteristic urban feature of Pezinok. Similar to these buildings is the native house of Ján Kupecký who became world famous as a very gifted and successful portraitist. Any visitors hungering for fine art shouldn't really forgo Schaubmar's Mill, which is located near the town in the borough of Cajla. The mill is both a cultural and technical monument, and includes the Gallery Naďve Painting, the one and only such a gallery in Slovakia. Here we can admire a collection of almost 100 paintings and sculptures by both Slovak and foreign masters. In addition, part of the gallery gives us a chance to take a look at various tools and technical objects used in mills in the past.

No less interesting are Pezinok's sacral sights, anyway – Church of the Assumption from the 14th century; originally Renaissance-styled (now Baroque) Church of the Transfiguration from the 17th century; and the Evangelic church, which impresses with its simple elegance.

Unfortunately, the sometimes-insensitive urbanism tendencies of the 20th century left their negative traces in Pezinok, too. As a result the buildings in the centre of the town that went up relatively recently completely disrupted the town's historical image. However, the pleasant spirit of a vintage town hasn't vanished at all – Pezinok lives with the sun, hard work at the vineyards, as well as with the sweet taste of maturing grapes. A number of wine-related events, feasts, celebrations and wine markets all contribute to a very special atmosphere here.

LEFT PAGE
▲ One of the wine-cellars on famous Small Carpathian Wine Route
▼ Typical winegrowers' house

RIGHT PAGE
Courtyard of the Small Carpathian Museum of Wine-growing

Important milestones in the town's history
1208 – the first record of the town, being a property of Bratislava Castle
1376 – Pezinok was granted privileges enabling it to hold markets
1580 – the town was under the rule of the Illésházys
1647 – Pezinok became a free royal town

Famous personalities
Ján Kupecký (1667 – 1740), painter
Jozef Ľudovít Holuby (1836 – 1923), natural scientist
Zuzka Medveďová (1897 – 1985), painter
Eugen Suchoň (1901 – 1993), composer
František Bokes (1906 – 1968), historian
Imrich Hornáček (1925 – 1977), publicist

Places and sights worth visiting
Birthplace of Ján Kupecký
Burgher houses along the sides of the square
Church of the Assumption
Church of the Transfiguration
Evangelical church
Monastery and Church of the Holy Trinity
Pezinok's chateau
Schaubmar's Mill
Small-Carpathian Museum of Winegrowing
Town Hall
Town walls

PIEŠŤANY

Mud Worth Gold

Every spring, the parks in the town of Piešťany are in bloom. Tulips, magnolias, platans and many other beautiful flowers and trees welcome visitors who came here in search of lost health. Medicinal thermal water and the famous curative mud in the local spa was described already in 1642 in a Latin poem 'Hymn to the Spa in Piešťany' by Czech poet Adam Trajan, an expellee who worked as a vicar in the nearby village of Drahovce. Many years later, the well-known Slovak writer Gejza Vámoš worked here as a doctor; one of the greatest Slovak poets ever, Ivan Krasko, spent the last years of his life here, and playwright Ivan Stodola lived here for a certain period. As if the oasis of peace that this spa town provides was giving power to these artistic souls...

The emergence of the local spa is connected with a legend about a peacock. The legend has it that local people spotted the peacock putting its wounded leg into the mud pit near the Váh River that flows through the

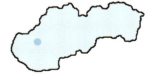

Important milestones in the town's history
1113 – the first written record
1642 – Piešťany gained the status of a town
1933 – construction of Colonnaded Bridge took place

Famous personalities
Adam Trajan (1586 –1650), poet, vicar
Ivan Krasko (1845 – 1958), poet
Ivan Stodola (1888 – 1977), playwright
Gejza Vámoš (1901 – 1956), doctor, writer

Places and sights worth visiting
Colonnaded Bridge
Spa Island
St. Stephen's Church
The Museum of Balneology

town. Only much later they realised that the mud here is special and curative.

The first official written record of Piešťany being inhabited comes from 1113, but it wasn't until 1642 that the town was granted status as a town. However, according to archaeological findings available, people knew about the hot springs even in prehistoric times. A prehistoric sculpture found in the nearby village of Moravany nad Váhom bears witness to this. The tiny sculpture, made of a mammoth tusk, was given the name 'Moravianska venuša' (Venus of Moravany), and is estimated to be 22,860 years old. If you want to admire it, you need to visit Bratislava Castle, where it's part of the permanent exposition.

The first owners of the spa in Piešťany were the Erdödys, who built a spa house here known as the Napoleonic Spa in 1822. The name reflects the fact that soldiers returning from Napoleonic wars used to visit it occasionally. However, the greatest glory for the spa came with the arrival of the Winters (another noble family), who had several Secession hotels built here, such as Hotel Royal, Thermia Palace, Pro Patria and Excelsior.

Towards the end of the 20th century, more spa houses went up – Balnea Palace, Balnea Grand, Balnea Splendid and Balnea Esplanade. In addition, the whole spa area was finished, including Spa Island, the scenery of which is made up of sculptures and fountains scattered around the park. The most famous embellishment of the Colonnaded

Bridge is the Kuhmayer sculpture known as Crutch-breaker, which is adored by all spa visitors and tourists to the town. The list of 'celebrity' visitors provides an indication of just how popular the spa in Piešťany is around the world. Austrian-Hungarian Emperor Franz Joseph with his wife Elisabeth (called Sisi), German Emperor William II, painter Alfonz Mucha, Indian maharajahs, Russian opera singer Fyodor Shalyapin, famous Czech actor Vlasta Burian, and many others have visited the Piešťany spa. Not only visits by famous people, but also the complete history of spa in Piešťany is well documented in the Museum of Balneology, located in the spa vestibule.

Two bridges connect the spa area and the downtown – Colonnaded Bridge (constructed in 1933 according to a design by famous architect Emil Belluš), and Krajinský Bridge.

The sacral sights in Piešťany include parts of a formerly Gothic church and monastery, as well as Classicist Church of St. Stephen (dating as back as early 19th century).

Not far from Piešťany, in Moravany, you have a chance to visit a Renaissance chateau built by Bishop Csáky at the end of the 16th century. During the 1960s, the chateau was restored, and since then it serves as a place where graphic artists from all around the world meet annually. When the meetings are held, many of their works (paintings, sculptures) are installed in the chateau's interior and in the park outside, which gives you an impression of visiting a captivating gallery.

LEFT PAGE

◄ Thermia Palace spa house, built by spa owners – the Winters.

▲ Captivating scenery on Spa Island

▼ Well-known sculpture of Crutch-breaker adorns the Colonnaded Bridge.

RIGHT PAGE

▲ The old, so-called Napoleonic spa was built in 1822.

▼ Colonnaded Bridge

SENICA

The Silky Centre of Sandy Region

There are many jokes running around concerning the area situated in western Slovakia near the border with the Czech Republic - Záhorie. The jokes are especially funny when interpreted with an understanding of the colloquial local dialect.

The name of the region comes from Latin, being derived from the term *Processus transmontanus*, which means '(the land) behind the mountains', which is in turn literally translated into Slovak expression 'Záhorie'. The region of Záhorie, the centre of which is Senica, is characterised by solitary cottages and houses spread as if randomly around the countryside. The land here is flat and arenaceous. In ancient and medieval times, the region was crossed by important trade routes leading down to the Carpathians through various passes. The routes were used by caravans carrying valuable goods, as well as hunters, soldiers, lords, bandits, merchants offering amber, salt, gold, furs, but also merchants selling servants...

Anyway, let's get back to the 11th century, when rulers created the so-called *confinium* exactly in this area of Slovakia. It was a border belt formed by thick forests. Later, the southern parts of today's Záhorie were hosted nomadic tribes related to Hungarians that set up a network of guard fortresses in the southern parts of what is today Senica - the best known of which were Korlát, Ostrý Kameň and Plavecký Castle. The lands around Senica belonged to the northern part of Halič principality, which later merged into Nitra County, and Castle Branč became the dominant site here.

Senica was part of the castle's domain. The first known lords here were the Abos in the second half of the 13th century. In the beginning of the 14th century, the castle and the town got a new owner, Matúš

Čák (of Trenčín), whose name is connected with the so-called 'glorious era' in many Slovak towns, as he successfully warded off all possible threats and raids.

In 1387, the era of King Sigmund Luxemburg began. The king donated Castle Branč and the lands around it to a feudal lord Stibor of Stiborice in 1394. During Stibor's rule, Senica was granted a set of town privileges, which guaranteed it a remarkable degree of economic independence.

The beginning of modern times brought a new owner to the castle and the whole domain - the noble family of the Nyáryovecs and their heirs by customs. The greatest manifestations of cultural life in the town were then represented by religion and education activities. Senica had a beautiful church built already in 1560, with religious ceremonies and divine services practised following Catholic rites and customs. Ten years later, the Nyáryovecs became attached to the ideas of the Reformation Movement, making way for a new religious faith to come to Senica.

Naturally, the history of Senica was influenced by the most important events of the 17th century - including Turkish invasions, anti-Hapsburg uprisings, as well as the struggle between the spiritual, ideological movements of Reformation and Counterreformation.

In the 18th century, Senica belonged to three towns economically most developed in Nitra County. Especially thriving was the local cloth manufacturer. After WWI, Senica opened a factory for production of synthetic fibres that made the town famous and uplifted it economically.

When it comes to secular sights in Senica, two manor houses are the highlights. The first one, built in the late-Baroque spirit (according to a project by F. A. Hill-

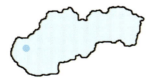

Important milestones in the town's history
between 1251 and 1261 – Castle Branč was being built
1256 – the first record of Senica

1332 – King Robert obtained the castle and the surrounding lands
1394 – Sigmund Luxemburg donated the castle and the lands to Count Stibor
1396 – Senica was granted town privileges
1614 – riot against local lords took place
1920 – factory to manufacture synthetic fibres was established

Famous personalities
Jozef Karol Viktorin (1822 – 1875), publisher
Viliam Pauliny-Tóth (1826 – 1877), writer, politician
Pavol Országh Hviezdoslav (1849 – 1921), poet, dramatist
Vladimír Fajnor (1875 – 1952), politician

Laco Novomeský (1904 – 1976), poet, politician
Ján Mudroch (1909 – 1968), painter
Svetozár Hurban Vajanský, writer, politician
Ján Hollý, poet

Places and sights worth visiting
Church of Madonna Visiting
Evangelical church
Gothic chapel
Manor house by F. A. Hillebrandt
Manor house by Ignatz Feigler Jr.
Ruins of Branč Castle
Synagogue
Záhorská Gallery

ebrandt) and finished in 1760, is a typical Theresian two-storey building with three wings. The manor has a mansard roof, large portal and a large main hall with columns along the sides. Nowadays it is the seat of Záhorská Gallery. Ignatz Feigler Jr. designed the other manor house in the late-Classicist style.

As for sacral buildings in the town, the most dominant is Church of Madonna Visiting. It was built in 1631 as a Protes-

tant church in the place of former Gothic church, but in 1654 it turned into a Catholic sanctuary. A Gothic chapel stands next to the church. Another church is Evangelical, the construction of which was finished in 1784. The local Jewish community has a Synagogue building (1866).

Unfortunately, the aforementioned Castle Branč fell into ruins but you can visit them in the vicinity of the nearby village of Podbranč.

SKALICA

The Town of Ruby

In Skalica, on a low hill on the outskirts of the town, stands St. George's Rotunda. Among the most beautiful Romanesque buildings in Slovakia and the town's dominant sight, St. George's was built around the 12th century as a castle church, and the only parts of its structure that have survived to date are the semicircular sanctuary and the circular aisle. When the town walls were being built in the 15th century, the rotunda was amended to become part of the fortification. Inside the rotunda, you can admire Gothic wall paintings that feature St. George fighting a dragon. Parts of the town walls (including the gate) are still standing near the rotunda - which is a solid evidence of Skalica having been a royal town in the past. Hungarian King Louis I the Great granted this prestigious privilege to the town on October 6, 1372. Thanks to further privileges (bestowed by King Sigmund Luxemburg) Skalica became an important economic, cultural and spiritual centre of the area in the centuries to come. The town represented a prosperous ground for various craftsmen, who were gathering into guilds and successfully did business here. The local drapers were especially famous all around the kingdom.

Also well-known were Skalica's winegrowers, who founded their fellowship ('Brotherhood of St. Urban') more than 300 years ago. Several historical monuments date back to this period - including the small Church of St. Urban (patron of winegrowers) and the altar with the winegrowers' blazon. Skalica was indeed made famous for its special variety of red wine - the Skalický rubín ('Skalica's Ruby'). Along with drinking this you must taste another local speciality - a sweet cake called 'trdelník'. The local vineyards, and the remarkably beautiful wineries and wine cellars, best illustrate the glory of wine growing.

Despite the sometimes-insensitive architectonic interventions, the centre of the town kept its original image to a large extent.

The centre's dominant site is a Gothic Roman Catholic Church of St. Michael, which was built not earlier than in 1372. Since then it underwent many restorations and facelifts, but some of its Gothic features and its Renaissance-styled tower have survived to date in their original form. Not far from the church stands the St. Ann's Chapel from the 15th century. Around the same time, another Gothic sanctuary - the Church of Our Lady (together with Franciscan monastery) - was built near the town walls. As early as in the first half of the 17th century, also Evangelists built their church with a monastery in Skalica, but their church was in early 19th century rebuilt into a hospital. Today's Evangelical church was erected in 1796 as a 'tolerance' church that had no tower. Famous Slovak architect Dušan Jurkovič was responsible for adding the tower in 1938.

The town offers some other interesting sacral sights - the Jesuit church with a monastery, the Calvary, the Marian Column on the square, and the synagogue building.

Besides living an active spiritual life, Skalica significantly went down in the nation's history books in the second half of the 19th century and in early 20th century. An anti-Magyarisation movement was organised here, and in 1918 - although

Important milestones in the town's history
1256 - first written record of Skalica
1372 - Skalica granted privileges of a free royal town
1918 - Skalica for several days the seat of caretaker Slovak government

Famous personalities
Augustin Doležal (1737 - 1802), writer
Jozef Škarnicel (1804 - 1877), letterpress printer
Daniel G. Lichard (1812 - 1882), editor

František Víťazoslav Sasinek (1830 - 1914), historian
Dušan Jurkovič (1868 - 1947), architect
Ľudovít Okánik (1869 - 1944), writer
Jozef Hollý (1879 - 1912), playwright
Gustáv Malý (1879 - 1952), painter
Janko Blaho (1901 - 1985), singer
František Krištof Veselý (1903 - 1977), singer and actor
Ľudovít Novák (1908 - 1992), linguist
Pavol Bunčák (1915 - 200), poet

Places and sights worth visiting
Church of Our Lady
Evangelical church
Franciscan monastery
Museum of Záhorie
St. Ann's Chapel
St. George's Rotunda
St. Michael's Church

LEFT PAGE

▲ Wall painting inside the Gothic St. Michael's Church

▼ Church of Our Lady of Seven Sorrows in Šaštín-Stráže, promoted to basilica minor

RIGHT PAGE

▲ St. George's Rotunda – the most precious site in Skalica, and the town's symbol

▼ Secession building of the House of Culture designed by famous Slovak architect Dušan Jurkovič

for several days only – Skalica became the seat of a caretaker Slovak government, which was unsuccessfully trying to negotiate removal of Hungarian troops from Slovakia. These important historical events were taking place behind the walls of secular buildings, especially the Town Hall. It was built in the beginning of the 17th century in late-Renaissance style, but in the latter half of the 19th century one floor was added and it was given a Classicist façade. When you're on the square, you simply can't overlook the beautiful Secession building of the House of Culture, which is now the seat of the Museum of Záhorie. The building was designed by architect Dušan Jurkovič and

built in 1905, and its front features a mosaic inspired by the drawings of Czech graphic artist Mikoláš Aleš. Another interesting building – Renaissance-styled Gvadány's Curia – today houses the municipal library.

If you're trotting around Skalica and you're hungry for more sacral sites, you should definitely visit a nearby pilgrimage destination called Šaštín-Stráže. The local Statue of Our Lady of Seven Sorrows was proclaimed to be miraculous, and this was confirmed even by a papal decree issued by Pope Urban VIII. For this reason, thousands of the faithful frequent the site, elevated in 1964 by Pope Paul VI to the status of basilica minor.

ŠTÚROVO

The Southernmost Natural Beauty in Slovakia

On the left bank of the Danube, in the southern part of the Podunajská Wold, lies the town of Štúrovo, which has at least two superlatives - it's the southernmost and the hottest town in Slovakia.

Its location and beautiful scenery attract visitors, especially in summer. Paying a visit to this area is really worth it - you can admire the vista of a lovely meander of the Danube (which is a natural Slovakia's border with Hungary). At the same time you can enjoy a breathtaking view of the basilica in Esztergom on the Hungarian bank of the river.

The rich history of Štúrovo is, quite naturally, closely connected with the town of Esztergom and its basilica. In the mid-20th century, extensive archaeological research was carried out on the local banks of the Danube, discovering a very old (some 5,000 years) settlement, which proves that this area had been populated since time immemorial.

During the Roman Empire, a settlement called Solva occupied the area of today's Esztergom, and the left bank (i.e. the place of today's Štúrovo) was a site of a military camp Anavum.

First written records of the town, which was then actually somewhat of a village called Kakath, come from a document issued in 1075. The document has it that the ruler gave the local monastery ten ferrymen's houses and a part of the local lands. The town presumably originated from a merger of the settlements Nána and Kakath, later changing its name to Parkan.

When Turks in 1541 captured the city of Budín, the fate of Hungarian Kingdom (in which today's Slovakia was included) was for the next 150 years consigned to plundering, raiding, devastation and wars. Hungary was perpetually trying to get rid of Turkish dominance as well as the rule of Hapsburgs in the kingdom.

In 1543, Turks managed to conquer Esztergom, and subsequently took control of Kakath. Of course, they realised Kakath's strategic advantage, so they built a fortification where the Roman Catholic Church stands today. Together with Esztergom,

Important milestones of the town's history
1075 – oldest written record on a settlement called Kakath
1241 – settlement is referred to as Parkan
1543 – Esztergom was conquered by Turkish armies
1724 – village was promoted to town having a privilege to hold fairs
1895 – bridge linking Parkan and Esztergom was built
2001 – Maria Valeria's Bridge was reopened

Places and sights worth visiting
Calvary
Church of St. Imrich
Vadaš (open-air swimming pool)

Parkan became an important point for Turks, as they could comfortably set out on their further invasions from here. In 1724, the village was promoted to a town with the right to hold fairs. The town gained another set of privileges from Empress Maria Therese in 1740.

In 1895, the bridge over the Danube, linking Parkan and Esztergom, was built and given name the Bridge of Maria Valeria. The bridge, destroyed during WWII in 1944, had to be reconstructed in late 20th century, and was opened to public in 2001. Now it serves as one of Slovak-Hungarian border crossings.

The late-Baroque Roman Catholic Church of St. Imrich is an attraction for visitors to the southernmost town in Slo-

vakia. Built in 1701, its interior has precious altar paintings, a pulpit with paintings of four gospellers and an organ-case from 1790. The church complex also includes the late-Baroque Calvary that dates back to 1766.

Perhaps the greatest attraction for holidaymakers (especially families with kids) coming to Štúrovo in summer is the open-air swimming pool Vadaš – the largest swimming pool in Slovakia. The river channels of the Hron, joining the Danube behind the town, are a real paradise for fishermen.

The river twists and turns in majestic swoops across the flat landscape which, given the lack of a prominent hill, can best be appreciated from an aerial perspective.

LEFT PAGE

▲ The square is replete with burgher houses.

▼ The remains of a Roman camp in the village of Iža

◄ Late-Baroque Roman Catholic church

RIGHT PAGE

Maria Valeria Bridge connects Štúrovo and Esztergom

TOPOĽČANY

The Town Brewing the Best Beer

Once there was a settlement situated on a high terrace next to the Nitra River in the locality simply called Hrad ('Fort'). Between the Stone Age and medieval times, the settlement several times changed both its size and location, as it had to adapt itself to natural circumstances. The area was lined by two rivers: the Bebrava and the Nitra; and historians nowadays assume that the process of population in this area culminated in the middle of the 9th century. This is how Topoľčany came into existence - the town that was called after poplar trees, so typical for the Upper Nitra area.

The advantageous location of Topoľčany, nested in the vicinity of a junction of important long-distance routes, ensured that the town was already prosperous during the 11th century, when it became a market-and-customs town and a parish seat, and the first known record of Topoľčany dates back to 1173. Topoľčany and its closest surroundings belonged under royal properties until King Belo III took the throne. In 1342, King Charles Robert promoted it to become a royal town, and soon after, Topoľčany received new owners - the noble family of Čáks. The famous family, historically the best known member of which was Matúš Čák of Trenčín, was in need of a fortified centre, but the flatland around Topoľčany wasn't suitable for building such a site. That's why they decided to build the castle (today known as Topoľčany Castle) far away from the town. Today, we can see only its ruins, located above the village of Podhradie. Throughout the 13th century, the castle was the centre of the Topoľčiany domain. For a few years in the 15th century, the town - including the castle - was raided, conquered and held by the Hussites. The castle also had an important defence function during the Turkish in-

vasions. It resisted all these incursions, but suffered some losses too. The greatest damage was caused by the imperial army during Rákóczi's (anti-Hapsburg) Uprising in early 18th century. Though it was restored later, it was gradually crumbling. Today, the castle's dominant features are the main tower, built in Romantic style, and a fortification that is relatively well preserved.

Topoľčany was prosperous also thanks to building of a post office on the Via Magna route. Via Magna was finished in 1550 as one of the longest transportation routes in the Hungarian Empire. It used to connect Vienna and the empire's cities like Košice, Debreczen and Sibia. In the late medieval period, Topoľčany ranked among the bigger towns, comparable to Nitra, for example.

In 1601, Topoľčany became the property of a famous aristocratic family of the Forgáčs, which - thanks to their good connections to the king - helped the town to be granted a royal privilege of holding markets. The years to come were not so beneficent to the town, however. Even though this was a tough period, full of various catastrophes and disasters, development of Topoľčany didn't stop. People lived on farming and cattle breeding, and crafts were at first also related to farming activities. Among the oldest crafts in the town were the flour miller's trade, leather processing and smiths of various kinds. With crafts gradually taking over, craftsmen began to associate themselves into guilds. The oldest guilds were, for example, those of shoemakers, tailors, girdlers, button makers, furriers and haberdashers. The greatest boom for crafts came in the 18th century. In those days, as many as a hundred craftsmen's workshops were active in the town. Even the famous Slovak polymath Matej Bel recorded Topoľčany as

Important milestones in the town's history
1173 – the first written record of a settlement existing in the area of today's Topoľčany
1334 – the first account of Topoľčany being referred to as a town
1342 – Topoľčany was promoted to a royal town
1599 – the town gained the privilege to hold markets
1787 – an extensive fire hit the town

1831 – Topoľčany suffered from cholera epidemics
1870 – sugar refinery was built in Topoľčany
1882 – railway was built to cross the town

Famous personalities
Ján Romanovský (1916 – 1989), writer
Ivan Sulík (1943), literary critic

Places and sights worth visiting
Chateau in Tovarniky
Geographic Museum
Roman Catholic Church
Topoľčany Castle

LEFT PAGE
Ruins of Topoľčany Castle at the village of Podhradie

RIGHT PAGE
▲ Chateau and its park, in the town precinct Továrniky, are built in Baroque style.
◄ Tríbeč Museum
► Town square
▼ Church of the Assumption

a 'town with remarkably developed farming and fruit growing, where many craftsmen live'. Topoľčany's beer and bread are said to have been famous even then.

Topoľčany was a serf town, but its citizens were proudly calling it Veľké Topoľčany ('Big Topoľčany') – although the town's centre only consisted of a small square and two or three streets around it. Most of the houses in the town were ground floor only, built from clay bricks. The exceptions were only three important buildings: District House, the Town Hall and the post office. Some more sumptuous townhouses were built in the late 19th centu-

ry after Topoľčany became a district seat of some greater importance.

The most significant sights in the town include a Baroque church (which dates back to 1740) and a Baroque chateau situated in the town borough called Tovarníky (built in mid-18th century upon the foundations of a 17th-century Renaissance building).

Nowadays, Topoľčany is perhaps best known thanks to its beer (branded Topvar), which belongs to the top beers in Slovakia, especially because of the area's very favourable climate in terms of growing the primary commodities that are used in brewing.

TRENČIANSKE TEPLICE

Carpathian Jewel

Who knows what brings fame to bridges over rivers – maybe it's their architects and builders. There's a bridge in Slovakia that has brought fame not only to the town where it overarches a small river but to the whole country as well. It's the Bridge of Fame in the small town of Trenčianske Teplice. The biggest film festival in Slovakia, Art Film, is held in this splendid spa town early in the summer annually. This international festival of art films and films about artists is a place where film stars meet – actors, actresses, film directors, producers and many others who work in the world of movies. And it's the Bridge of Fame where a plate dedicated to the top guest of the festival is added. The plates given here to date include those dedicated to Sophia Loren, Gina Lollobrigida, Franco Nero, Ornella Muti, as well as exceptional Slovak film actors and actresses – Jozef Kroner and Emília Vášáryová, for example.

Long before the era of the successful film festival was kicked off, Trenčianske Teplice, situated only a few kilometres away from the city of Trenčín, became famous as a spa resort. The town is nestled amid lovely nature in the Teplička Valley, and thanks to this exceptional location and the healing springs it was given a Romantic attribute – 'Carpathian Jewel'. When lords of Trenčín Castle learned about this natural jewel in the past, they discovered that it's worth not only being protected, but also aggrandised. Palatine Štefan Zápoľský in the 16th century laid the foundation stone of what later became the spa resort area. The spa is open year round, and is visited by people looking for a cure for diseases of locomotive organs

and the nervous system. The resort lies in an ideal natural environment, protected against wind and enjoying many sunny days. Traditional curative methods have been marvellously joined by the modern methods of comprehensive balneotherapy. This features the use of curative effects of thermal mineral springs along with wonderful healing effects of mineralised mud. Thermal water rises from the depth of around 1,200 metres, and before it comes out on the surface, it flows through limy soil and layers of magnesium, which results in its intense mineralization and warming.

Besides enjoying the beneficial effects of the healing springs, visitors to the spa have a chance to admire an interesting architecture of the spa houses in Trenčianske Teplice. The most popular is the bath called Hammam, which you can take in the spa house called Sina. This spa house is decorated in an Oriental (Arabic-Moorish) style of late 19th century. The spa house includes a bandstand that dates back to 1932. What definitely can't be overlooked here is the lovely ornamented arcade. Not far away from here, you can enter a church from the early 20th century, inside which you can admire the carved wooden ceiling. The surroundings of the spa houses are glamorised by a Romantic English park with a small pond.

It's said that the best view of a country one can get is from a horse's back. You have a great chance to do so when you're trotting around Trenčianske Teplice, because you have an opportunity to visit a famous horse-breeding farm in the nearby village of Motešice.

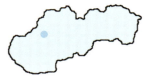

Important milestones in the town's history
1379 – first mention of thermal springs
1598 – first record on Trenčianske Teplice itself

Famous personalities
Andrej Bagar (1900 – 1966), theatre actor and director

Places and sights worth visiting
Bridge of Fame
Horse-breeding farm in the village of Motešice
Spa area
Thermal pool Zelená žaba ('Green Frog')

LEFT PAGE
▲ Bath Hammam, in the spa house called Sina, is decorated in an Oriental style.
▼ The spa promenade

RIGHT PAGE
◄ Oriental details of the Hammam bath
► Hammam spa house
▼ Atlantis spa house

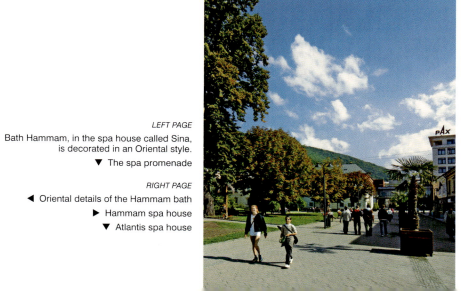

TRENČÍN

Legendary City of Fights and Loves

Like Nitra, the city of Trenčín is also legendary in Slovak history. The only difference is in the fact that Nitra symbolises the legend of a spiritual message delivered by old Slavs, while Trenčín is emblazoned with legends of rebellion and military power. Indeed, many European rulers sought the Hungarian royal crown, but the real power was always in the hands of 'uncrowned' kings. For example, Matúš Čák of Trenčín, being opposed to the royal family of the Anjous, faced off against the will of the pope, and ruled boundlessly. Regardless of what legends say, this nobleman from Trenčín represents the greatest symbol of power and rebellion against Hungarian aristocracy, on which even royal powers depended in Hungary. His name will always remain linked with Slovakia's history, but particularly with the history of regions along the Váh River and, naturally, with Trenčín.

To follow the traces to the oldest history of this region, we need to begin somewhere much earlier than in the era of Matúš Čák, because archaeological findings bear witness to the area having been populated already in the Stone Age. Unique historical evidence is available from the beginning of the AD giving us proof of Roman population in this area. At that time, Romans were expanding towards the Danube. In order to move the borders of their empire as far as possible, they were gradually founding military camps further and further afield, and one of these settlements, called Laugaricio (Latin), or Leukaristos (Greek), was built in Trenčín. An inscription on the rock below Trenčín Castle known today as the *Roman Inscription* was carved in 179 A.D. It commemorates the Roman victory over Germanic tribes, and reads: 'To commemorate the victory of emperors – Roman troops camping down here in Laugaricio – 855 soldiers of the second legion – Maximianus, the legate of the second administrative legion, had this writing inscribed.' This is a solid (and also the oldest written in Slovakia) evidence of the northern-most presence of expansive Roman troops in central Europe. The expansion concerned was taking place during the reign of Roman Emperor Marcus Aurelius.

The area along the Váh River, where Trenčín is the biggest city today, became part of the Hungarian Empire in the 11th century. At that time, Trenčín had considerable status – it was the centre of the region and the seat of regional administrative bodies in their simple form. In documents dated 1111 we find records of a settlement nested under a massive castle and situated along an old trade route (the famous Jasper Route). The settlement was scourged by Tatars in 1241, so the first signs of a real development in Trenčín could be seen only in the 13th century, when it became the property of the noble family of Čáks.

The town gained most of its fame during the era of Matúš Čák, who became ruler of nearly the whole area of today's Slovakia, owning around 30 castles around the country. Trenčín gained quite a wide range of various privileges over the medieval period, and King Sigmund Luxemburg in 1412 promoted it to become a free royal town. It had a key position in terms of defending the area against the Hussite incursions. Matúš Čák of Trenčín – 'Lord of the Váh and the Tatras' – turned the castle into an almost unconquera-

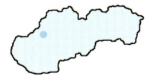

Important milestones in the city's history

179 A.D. – Roman Inscription put on the rock below the Trenčín Castle
1111 – first written record of local settlement
1241 – town raided by Tatars
1324 – Trenčín granted town privileges
1412 – town promoted to a free royal town
1708 – fire, flood, the plague

Famous personalities

Matúš Čák Trenčiansky (circa 1260 – 1321), ruler over Slovak lands
Šimon Jesenský (1529 – 1596), teacher
Ján Hadík (1631 – 1681), poet
Alexander Ľudovít Mičátek (1837 – 1914), lexicographer
Miloš Alexander Bazovský (1899 – 1968), painter
Štefánia Pártošová (1913 – 1987), writer
Vojtech Bárdoš (1914 – 1982), doctor
Vojtech Zamarovský (1919 – 2006), historian, historical non-fiction writer
Viliam Klimáček (1958), playwright

Places and sights worth visiting

Church of František Xaverský
Evangelical church
Gallery of M. A. Bazovský
Notre Dame Church
Parish Church of the Virgin Mary
Parish staircase
Regional House
St. Ann's Chapel
Synagogue
Town Gate
Trenčín Castle
Trenčín Museum

LEFT PAGE
Municipal Tower

RIGHT PAGE
▲ Legendary Trenčín Castle and Church of the Virgin Mary
▼ The 'rock upon the Váh' is a well-known tourist destination

51

ble fortress, and had another palace (known as Palace of Matúš) annexed to the castle.

The decades to come were much worse – for both the castle and the town. Following the plundering of the town (by the imperial armies commanded by General Johan Katzianer) and the big fire of 1528, many sites had to be restored, remodelled, rebuilt, or even completely re-erected. Then, in the spirit of Renaissance, Parish Church of the Virgin Mary was restored, and new houses were erected on the town's square. In the latter half of the 16th century, houses with arcades were added here; however, these were later completely restored, unfortunately. Under the influence of recatholisation movement, Trenčín's dominant architectonic style changed in the 17th century, when Jesuits built an extensive church-and-monastery complex known as the Church of František Xaverský. The 18th century also left traces, mostly negative, on the appearance of the town and the look of the castle. Local people were trembling before the Turks and, in addition, they lived in constant fear of struggles between the imperial court and Hungarian aristocratic insurgents. Of course, the town was unable to avoid natural disasters. Particularly disastrous was 1708 – firstly, an extensive fire burst out; secondly, there came a great flood; and thirdly, a wave of ghastly plague epidemics struck Trenčín. A memorial to these thorny days is the Trinity Column, the dominant site on today's Mierové Square.

Another important landmark in Trenčín's history was 1790 – a big fire hit the town again, this time including the castle. A series of restorations, repairs and rebuilding projects had to be carried out again and the look of the town completely changed. Trenčín was given a strong, accentuated Classicist image.

Of the original two gates in Trenčín's city walls only the upper one (which used to be called the 'Turkish Gate') has survived to date. The church-and-monastery complex, originally Jesuit and later Piarist, had to undergo restorations. These sacral buildings create a unique symbiosis of architecture, painting, statuary and artistic stucco decorations. Inside, painting on the ceiling belongs among the most brilliant achievements in terms of wall paintings from the Baroque period in Slovakia. The complex nowadays houses the Gallery of M. A. Bazovský, carrying the name after one of the best modern painters in Slovakia. The so-called Regional House (in Slovak: 'Župný dom'), in which the Trenčín Museum is installed since 1939, deserves a visit – as does Trenčín's Jewish synagogue, which has neo-Romantic look, but several Oriental features can be spotted on it, too.

Today, Trenčín is a modern city, but it doesn't forget about its past. Even young people from the city usually know a lot about Trenčín's history, including the most famous native (Matúš Čák) and the most famous local legend (a romantic story of undying love of Omar and Fatima).

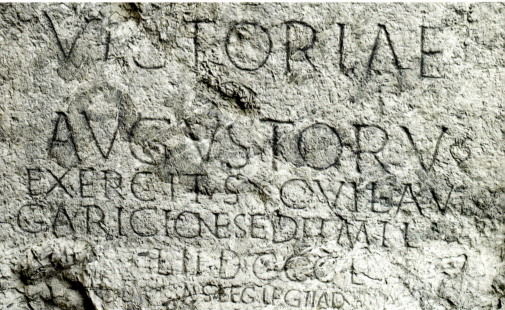

TRNAVA

Slovakia's Little Rome

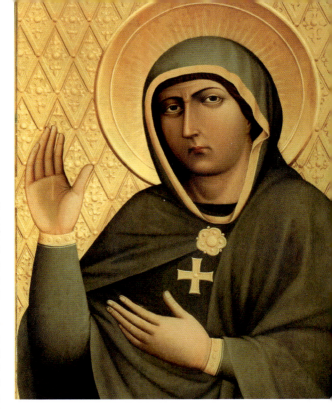

To every Slovak, Trnava connotes churches. Quite legitimately, as this western Slovak city, with its numerous sacral sights, and especially eleven Roman Catholic churches, an evangelistic church and a synagogue, belongs among the truly unique places in Slovakia. It is assumed that Trnava was born in the late 9th century as a market settlement on the junction of trade routes. However, many archaeological findings from the Neolithic era indicate that it was much earlier. Some more tangible evidence on Trnava dates back to 1211, with references to 1205. Anyway, the most important – and historically the most valuable – artefact is a paper by Hungarian King Belo IV from 1238, which speaks of Trnava being granted free royal town privileges. This is when Trnava began to record its 'urban' history and the town started to live its 'urban' life. This, of course, required handling the security of people living in it, so as early as in the mid-13th century Trnava began to fortify itself, and its town walls, bulwarks, ramparts, ditches, fosses and moats (shaping up the town's ingenious water defence) made it an almost invincible fortress. A number of ecclesiastical institutions and orders were seated here in medieval times, enabling the town to provide a cosy and hospitable abode for Hungarian kings when holding important political or diplomatic talks.

The 16th century was the most important in the history of Trnava. It was then that the town turned into a 'city', becoming an important trade centre – even in terms of foreign trade it partially took over the function of Turk-occupied trade centres in the Hungarian Empire. Unlike other towns in the empire, Trnava was experiencing population growth and rapid development of crafts. When in 1543 Turks captured the city of Esztergom, the local bishop and his chapter moved to Trnava, which significantly set the tone for the city, making it for the following three centuries an important cultural and religious centre of the Hungarian Empire.

Important milestones in the town's history
1211 – the first written record on Trnava
1238 – King Belo IV granted free royal town privileges to Trnava
1543 – Esztergom archbishop and his chapter moved to Trnava
1635 – Trnava University was established
1777 – the university was moved from Trnava to Budin

1792 – Slovak Intellectual Journeymen's Institution was set up in Trnava
1846 – horse-drawn railway linking Bratislava and Trnava was finished
1870 – Fellowship of St. Vojtech was established
since 1978 – Trnava has been the seat of Slovakia's Archbishop-Metropolitan

Famous personalities
Ján Sambucus (1531 – 1584), central European humanist, philologist, doctor and historian
Juraj Papánek (1738 – 1802), important figure of the Age of Enlightenment, historian, author of early scientific works on history of Slovaks

Móric Beňovský (1746 – 1786), globetrotter, King of Madagascar
Ján Hollý (1785 – 1849), poet
Štefan Banič (1870 – 1940), inventor of parachute
Ján Koniarek (1878 – 1952), sculptor
Mikuláš Schneider-Trnavský (1881 – 1958), composer
Maximilián Schurmann (1890 – 1960), painter
Fraňo Štefunko (1903 – 1974), sculptor
Jozef Nižňánsky (1903 –1976), writer
Andrej Žarnov (1903 – 1982), poet
František Hečko (1905 – 1960), novelist
Martin Gregor (1906 – 1982), actor
Karol Elbert (1911 – 1997), composer
Anton Malatinský (1920 – 1992), football player and coach
William Schiffer (1920) – world-renown graphic artist

The 17th century wasn't so kind to Trnava, however. The city was constantly destroyed by frequent fires, suffered from epidemics, and witnessed uprisings of the Hungarian aristocracy against ruling Hapsburgs. The only positive year in the century was 1635, when Cardinal Peter Pázmáň established Trnava University. Although the university had a pan-Hungarian (and later even European) character, and the teaching language was Latin, half of the staff and students were Slovaks. Trnava as a university city was called 'the home of Pallas Athena', 'the seat of muses', 'the queen of wisdom', and 'Athens of the Hungarian Empire'. Unfortunately, in its prime time, in 1777, the university was moved to Budín and later to Budapest, based on the decision of the emperor. Some 50 years later the bishop, together with his chapter and even an archbishop, returned to Esztergom, but Trnava kept its cultural and spiritual traditions.

At the turn of the 18th and 19th centuries in Trnava, many national 'awakeners' met here, headed by Anton Bernolák. It was he who codified the western Slovak dialect as a standard Slovak language and in 1792 Bernolák, together with Juraj Fándly, set up the so-called 'Slovak Intellectual Journeymen's Institution' (in Slovak: Slovenské učené tovarišstvo), the aim of which was to spread the standard Slovak language.

Over the coming years, the city saw further economic development, but intellectual and spiritual life was somewhat halted during the 20th century. Architecture in the city was badly affected by the socialist era (1948-89), for example. Despite the state ignoring Trnava's spiritual dimension, the city became a bishopric seat in 1978, and has been a religious metropolis in Slovakia until today. Nowadays there are two universities here: Trnava University and the University of St. Constantine and Methodius.

Now let's take a look at the unique historical sights, as there are plenty of them to be seen in Trnava. Among the most sig-

Mária Prechovská (1921 – 1995), actress
Miroslav Válek (1927 – 1997), poet
Eva Kostolányiová (1942 – 1975), pop singer

Places and sights worth visiting
Archbishop's Palace
Basilica of St. John the Baptist
Church of Assumption
Church of St. Nicholas
Church of the Holy Trinity
Museum of Western Slovakia
St. Ann's Church
St. Helen's Church
St. James's Church

St. Joseph's Church
Synagogue status quo
Trojičné Square, featuring the sculptural group
of the Holy Trinity

LEFT PAGE
▲ Painting featuring 'Merciful Madonna of Trnava' in a
lovely Gothic sight – Church of St. Nicholas
◄ Interior of Roman Catholic Basilica
of St. John the Baptist
▶ Statue of the Immaculate, on top of Municipal Tower

RIGHT PAGE
◄ Pulpit in the Basilica of St. John the Baptist
is uniquely embellished
▶ One of the former hostels for students

nificant – both in Slovakia and Europe – are the aforementioned town walls. Only a few cities in the world can be proud of such long sections of its former fortification walls as have been preserved in the historical centre of Trnava.

The walls were originally 3-kilometre long, 10-metre high, 2.3 metres in thickness, and had 35 towers. Another dominant sight is the City Tower, built in a Gothic style by Master Jakub in 1574. The tower stands on the Trojičné Square, where you can also find the Theatre of Ján Palárik building, one of the oldest theatres in Slovakia. Roman Catholic University Basilica of St. John the Baptist definitely belongs among the most valuable sights in Trnava.

It was built between 1629 and 1637 as part of the complex of university buildings. Part of the area is the building of former Oláh's Seminary, in which we can nowadays find Museum of Books and History of Printing. An immensely valuable building is the three-aisle Roman Catholic parish Church of St. Nicholas, the construction of which was started in the latter half of the 14th century and finished around the mid-15th century. Between 1543 and 1820 it was a cathedral of Esztergom archbishops, and near the church stands the Archbishop's Palace. Archbishop Mikuláš Oláh had it built on some older Gothic foundations in 1562 to become his residence.

Even these days the palace keeps its original function – it serves as a seat of Slovakia's Archbishop-Metropolitan. Of the list of Trnava's sacral sights, you definitely shouldn't miss the following Roman Catholic churches: Holy Trinity (with a monastery), St. James's, St. Helen's, St. Joseph's, St. Ann's and Church of Assumption, which is linked with a Clarist monastery where the Museum of Western Slovakia is installed (since 1954). It includes collections of ceramics and clay ware, folk art objects, bells (the only collection in Slovakia) and documents on the history of the city and the university. Sacral sights in the city also include an Evangelical church for the faithful of Augsburg confession, and the synagogue with oriental features.

Not only Trnava itself, but also its surroundings are interesting and attractive. In the splendid environment of the eastern slopes of the Low Carpathians, and standing on the hillock amid an English park, we can find beautiful Smolenice Castle, which stands on the place of former castle from the 14th century. Its last owner Jozef Pálffy decided to have a new castle built upon the ruins, and the new one was intended to become Pálffy's feudal residence. Another highlight found near Trnava is the chateau in the village of Dolná Krupá, famous for having been visited by composer Ludwig van Beethoven, who composed his famous Moonlight Sonata here.

LEFT PAGE

Beautiful natural scenery featuring eastern slopes of Small Carpathians

RIGHT PAGE

▲ On the square, Church of St. Nicholas stands at the former site of a Romanesque church.

◀ Smolenice Castle stands on the hillock amidst an English park.

▶ Classicist chateau in the village of Dolná Krupá

◄▲ Unique altar in the Church of St. Nicholas

◄▼ St. James's Church gained its Baroque look at the turn of the 17th and 18th centuries.

►▲ Dominant feature of the square and the whole city is Municipal Tower, from where you can enjoy a lovely view.

►▼ Basilica of St. John the Baptist is one of Trnava's historical highlights.

Sculpture of David in the Basilica of St. John the Baptist

ZLATÉ MORAVCE

Gold in the Brook

Once the seat of Tekov district, nowadays a centre of Upper Žitava area – that's Zlaté Moravce, a town that had an important status already in the times of the Hungarian Empire.

The first written record comes from the Charter of Zobor (dated 1113) where it was

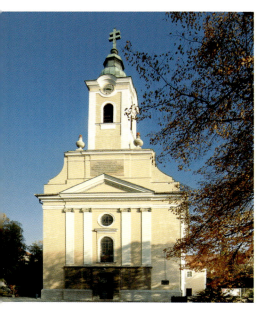

referred to as 'villa Morawa'. However, according to archaeologists, the area was populated much earlier.

A pyx (monstrance) made of ivory was found in a nearby village of Čierne Kľačany, which experts consider to have been a gift from Byzantine Emperor Michael III to his Great-Moravian counterpart. The original is kept in a treasury in Bratislava Castle, while a copy can be seen in the Church of St. Ján Nepomucký in Nitra.

Also interesting is the origin of the town's name. Historical documents include several names referring to it – Morowa, Marota, Marat, etc. It's difficult

to say which of them served as the prototype from which today's name was derived. Clearer is the origin of the attribute 'zlaté' (gold, golden). It's said that it was given to the town due to the fact that pieces of gold were found in the local brook. Again, we can't be sure if the story is true, but the fact is that since then the brook has been called Zlatňanka ('Gold Brook').

The history of Zlaté Moravce is full of events related to Turkish inroads. Turks burnt the town down in 1830, which only topped all the disasters that had been happening in Zlaté Moravce during previous centuries.

However, there were some bright moments, when Turkish threats were driven off, like the one in August 1652 when captain of the Nové Zámky fortress Adam Forgáč, who fought Turks near the village of Nové Vozokany, managed to repel them. The battle went down in history as the Battle of Vozokany. Losses were on both sides: 800 Turks and 100 Slovaks died here.

Zlaté Moravce was the seat of Tekov district, and the famous Slovak poet Janko Kráľ (member of the Štúr Movement) lived here. Following his early death, he was buried in the town's cemetery, but the place of his rest cannot be empirically identified these days.

Another famous personality whose name is closely connected with the town was Cardinal Krištof Bartolomej Migazzi, who bought the Zlaté Moravce domain in 1771. It was Migazzi who significantly endeavoured to rebuild the local manor house with park, and restore the Church of St. Michael the Archangel.

His name is also connected with the arboretum in the village of Mlyňany – a park with more than a hundred-year tra-

LEFT PAGE

◀ Classicist Church of St. Michael the Archangel

▶ Arboretum in Mlyňany

▼ Mausoleum of the Migazzios family, former owners of Zlaté Moravce domain.

RIGHT PAGE

▲ Topoľčianky chateau used to be a summer seat of Hapsburgs.

▼ After WWI the chateau in Topoľčianky was used as a presidential retreat.

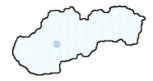

Important milestones in the town's history
1113 – the first written record of Zlaté Moravce – in the Charter of Zobor
1634 – the town was subdued by Turks
1652 – Battle of Vozokany took place
1720 – town was granted a privilege to hold fairs

Famous personalities
Juraj Selepčéni Pohronec (1595 – 1685), vicegerent of Hungary
Krištof Bartolomej Migazzi (1714 – 1803), cardinal
Andrej Radlinský (1817 – 1879), writer
Janko Kráľ (1822 – 1876), poet
Július Gábriš (1913 – 1987), archbishop

Places and sights worth visiting
Arboretum in Mlyňany
Chateau in Topoľčianky
Church of St. Michael the Archangel
Memorial to the Victory over Turks
Renaissance chateau
Župný House

dition, which belongs to the most valuable dendrological sites in Europe that sports greenery throughout the year.

Near Zlaté Moravce, in the village of Topoľčianky, we can find one of Slovakia's most important Classicist chateaux. It stands in the place of former Gothic water castle, which was later turned into a Renaissance fortress which was the seat of Tekov district between the 16th and the 18th centuries, when it played an important role in fighting Turks.

In the beginning of the 19th century, its new owner, Count Jozef Keglevich, had a part of it destroyed, and had a new wing annexed according to an architectonic project drawn by Luigi Pichl. This resulted in creation of a work that now belongs among the best examples of Classicist architecture in Slovakia.

The look of the chateau is even intensified by a Romantic English park, which fluidly merges into open space. In the past, the chateau was a summer seat of Hapsburgs, and after the WWI it was used as a presidential resort and, thus, Topoľčianky was frequented by the first president of Czechoslovakia, Tomáš Garrigue Masaryk. This is exactly where the book 'The Talks with T. G. Masaryk' (by famous Czech writer Karel Čapek) stemmed from.

The chateau includes a rare library, which contains more than 14,000 books and period printings. Impressive is also the interior, precious furnishing, paintings, ceramics and porcelain.

If you visit Topoľčianky, you shouldn't miss out paying a visit to the local horse-breeding farm Žrebčín Topoľčianky. Founded in 1921, it's the only state-owned stud farm in Slovakia. At the beginning of May, the farm traditionally commences its tourist, sports and breeding season.

BANSKÁ BYSTRICA

The City of Copper

The nature surrounding the city of Banská Bystrica deserves an attribute 'heavenly beautiful'.

Banská Bystrica, situated in the valley of the Hron River, is from one side lined by the rolling hills of the Low Tatras, and from the other side it's embraced by the Kremnické Mountains and the Bystrianska Highlands.

It's simply a magnificent area, to which the Creator was very generous - the real heart of Slovakia.

In the past, Banská Bystrica (which has the nickname 'the city of copper' due to extraction of copper ore taking place in local hills as early as the 14th century) has always been an important junction of trade routes.

Together with Banská Štiavnica and Kremnica, it has always belonged among the richest mining towns in central Slovakia. Banská Bystrica's long tradition of profitable mining helped it enjoy the favour of rulers, who granted it various special privileges that were usually given only to royal towns.

Considerable sums of money were flowing, too, to local lords, which motivated them to expand and develop the mines.

Among the biggest entrepreneurs in Banská Bystrica in the 15th century were German banker and merchant Jacob Fugger and Count of Spiš, Ján Thurzo. These two businessmen strengthened their positions through inter-family marriages, es-

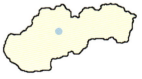

Important milestones in the city's history

1255 – first written reference to Banská Bystrica (in a document issued by Belo IV) – concerning the set of privileges related to extraction of gold, silver and other precious metals
1303 – the municipal hospital was built, along with Gothic Church of St. Elisabeth (the hospital burnt out in 1605)
1525 and 1926 – uprisings of miners
1761 – Banská Bystrica hit by a devastating fire
1944 – Slovak National Uprising (SNP) was kicked off in Banská Bystrica

1955 – Banská Bystrica's medieval historical core was proclaimed to be municipal memorial reserve

Famous personalities

Karol Ľudovit Libai (1816 – 1888), painter
Andrej Sládkovič (1820 – 1872), poet
Gustáv Kazimír Zachenter-Laskomerský (1824 – 1908), writer
Ján Botto (1829 – 1881), poet
Dominik Skutecký (1849 – 1921), painter
Terézia Vansová (1857 – 1942), writer
Jozef Murgaš (1864 – 1929), inventor of wireless telegraphy
Viliam Figuš-Bystrý (1875 – 1937), composer
Alexander Matuška (1910 – 1975), literary scientist
Paľo Bielik (1910 – 1983), actor and film director
Ján Bodenek (1911 – 1985), writer
Ján Cikker (1911 – 1989), music composer
Ivan Bukovčan (1921 – 1975), playwright

Places and sights worth visiting

Benický's House
Bishop's Palace
Ebner's House
Church of Our Lady
Church of St. Elisabeth
Church of St. František Xaverský
Clock Tower
Matej's House
Municipal Castle
Museum of Central Slovakia
National House
Old Town Hall
Slovak Church
SNP Memorial
Thurzo's House

tablishing a mining partnership – a world-renown corporation. In their mines they successfully introduced a new technology for smelting copper ore, which was a trade secret of Venetian companies that were the main buyers of the copper from Banská Bystrica.

Thanks to this, they soon took control of the world's copper market, and the copper from here can still be seen on many churches around Europe.

Anyway, nothing lasts forever, and the copper glory of Banská Bystrica is long gone. It was disturbed by a more competitive environment on the world's ore market (ores started to be massively imported from overseas), and the new business conditions resulted in local miners complaining about their living standards declining. These initial rumblings of discontent escalated to an uprising of miners from all mining towns in central Slovakia in 1525-1526.

All the aforementioned events influenced the architectonic activities, which best document the lives of people in Ban-

ská Bystrica. The oldest sight in the city is originally Romanesque, later Gothic, Church of Our Lady. The construction began in 1255 and inside the church today you can admire the late-Gothic Field Altar of St. Barbara, made by Master Paul of Levoča in 1509.

The church is a part of the Municipal Castle, which was built according to the model of Kremnica's Castle in the 15th century – by fortifying the areas around the church and the nearby cemetery. Administration buildings, Town Hall, Royal House and another church were built on this fortified site.

LEFT PAGE
▲ Miner's crest on Benický's House
◄ Burgher houses line the square on both sides.
► Municipal Castle

RIGHT PAGE
◄ Church of St. František Xaverský in the upper part of the square
► Interior of the Church of Our Lady

The Municipal Castle thus became the most important chamber, where municipal affairs were dealt with.

The fortification developed based on who represented the enemy for the rich Banská Bystrica. At first the castle was encircled only by mounds and palisades, and later the high stonewalls were built to fend off the frequent miners' riots.

In 1479, the so-called Matej's House was added to the northern side of the fortification – it was a seat of the royal administrator, which was given the name after King Matej's (Matthias Corvinius) coat of arms on the front face.

Further amendments to the castle's fortification were required due to the threat represented by Turkish raids in the 16th century. About one-fourth of the original fortification has survived to date, and three out of originally four bastions are still-standing today: the Parish Bastion, the Miners' Bastion, and the Scrivener's Bastion. Also the barbican has survived to date.

Villain riots also influenced architecture of sacral sights in Banská Bystrica. The Reformation Movement, spreading out from Germany, captured the poor at first.

However, all churches in the town were in the hands of Evangelists as of 1539. The Hapsburgs' Counterreformation in 1620 worsened relations between Catholics and Evangelists, meaning that the same churches in town were sometimes run by Catholics and sometimes Evangelists.

Walking up the spiral staircase, you get to the Bell Tower (also known as Slovakia's leaning tower – as that in Pisa, Italy), which was built in 1552 as a part of a municipal prison. During the last restoration works on it, taking place in the 18th century, the top of the tower diverted by as much as 40 centimetres, making the tower another European rarity. From the tower you have a nice view of SNP Square, which in recent years was turned

into a pedestrian zone, with a vibrantly pleasant atmosphere. The dominant site on the square is the Jesuit Church of St. František Xaverský. Also impressive here are some of the burgher houses, such as Thurzo's House, formerly known as 'Mittelhaus', now the Museum of Central Slovakia. Standing opposite it is Benický's House with an arcaded loggia, which houses a small art gallery.

Some other buildings here are also worthy of note – especially Bishop's Palace in the corner of the square, which in the latter half of the 19th century used to be the seat of Štefan Moyzes, Catholic Bishop and the first Chairman of Matica Slovenská. Another interesting site is the Bethlen's House, situated in the lower part of the square. It dates as far back as to the 14th century, and it was the place where the Hungarian Assembly (i.e. Parliament) in 1620 elected Count Gabriel Bethlen from Transylvania to become the Hungarian King.

LEFT PAGE
Late-Gothic St. Barbara's Field Altar, made by Master Paul of Levoča can be seen in the Church of Our Lady.

RIGHT PAGE
▲ Benický's House – dominant site on Banká Bystrica Square.
▼ Church of St. Elisabeth is on Dolná Street

BANSKÁ ŠTIAVNICA

Mining Land of Silver and Gold

Facades of many houses in the town of Banská Štiavnica are decorated with two lizards.

This is because the history of this famous mining town includes a tale of a shepherd who saw two lizards twinkle on a rock – one was silver and the other one golden. He tried to catch them, but the lizards were quick enough to hide beneath the rock. So the shepherd rolled the rock away, and suddenly he was dazzled by the resplendence of silver and gold ore lying below the rock.

Since then the two lizards have come to represent the symbol of the town, which is among the most splendid and romantic in Slovakia. Actually, not only in Slovakia – UNESCO in 1996 included the town on the World Heritage List.

The town grew out of the rocky hills of an inhospitable land. It's nestled on cascades of seven steep hills. Perhaps only thanks to rich deposits of silver and gold ore here, people were willing to cope with the environment and build houses here. Banská Štiavnica officially became a town during the rule of King Belo IV, who granted it with town privilege in 1238.

The greatest boom of the town was seen in the 15th century, when Banská Štiavnica remarkably changed its overall image. New sumptuous houses, as well as sacral and secular buildings appeared, all of them being very original thanks to the fact that they were built in an atypical environment.

Banská Štiavnica, with its steep streets, became the most extraordinary town in the whole Kingdom of Hungary. The town was unable to avoid military and religious tensions, as well as natural disasters causing great damage and loss, but – again, thanks to its wealth – it always managed to recover.

Italian architects, who participated on restorations of many burgher houses in the town, brought here an impressive beauty of the Renaissance style. Thanks to these masters many local buildings even nowadays boast interesting architectonic features which fully respect the uniqueness of this mountainous terrain. In the 17th century, an original site was built in the town - a wooden clapper, called *Klopačka*, which was used to call miners to come to work, or it was used for giving an alert signal when mining disasters or natural disasters took place.

When rumours started to spread, saying that the local mines would have to be closed, an expert in mining engineering J. K. Hell came to the town with an original plan to rescue the mines. His daring strategy wasn't trusted at first, so the project was submitted to King Charles VI, who eventually approved it. In line with Hell's project, more than 60 artificial mining water reservoirs were built around Banská Štiavnica. The system of

Important milestones in the town's history
1238 – Banská Štiavnica was granted town privileges
1735 – first mining school in Hungary was established in Banská Štiavnica
1762 – mining school was upgraded to become the Mining Academy – the Centre of Mining Theory and Practice in Europe
1993 – town was put on the UNESCO's List of World Cultural Heritage

Famous personalities
Pavol Rubigall (1510 – 1577), poet
Samuel Mikoviny (1700 – 1750), astronomer and cartographer
Jozef Karol Hell (1713 – 1789), constructor and inventor
Andrej Radlinský (1817 – 1879), writer and publisher
Andrej Sládkovič (1820 – 1872), poet
Andrej Kmeť (1841 – 1908), natural scientist
Jaroslav Augusta (1878 – 1970), painter
Edmund Gwerk (1895 – 1956), painter
Jozef Kollár (1899 – 1982), painter
Ľudovít Kneppo (1903 – 1983), electro technician
Ján Gonda (1905 – 1993), engineer
Jozef Horák (1907 – 1974), writer

Mining Academy hosted the following famous teachers:
J. M. Jacquin, J. A. Scopoli, A. Ruprecht, J. T. Peithner, M. Poda, K. Thierenberger, K. T. Delius, Möhling and Reichetzer.

Places and sights worth visiting
Burgher houses on Trinity Square
Calvary
Church of the Virgin Mary of the Snow – Frauenberg
Evangelical church
Former Dominican church with the remains of a monastery
Klopačka (a wooden clapper)
Marian column – Immaculata
New Castle
Old Castle
Roman Catholic Church of St. Catherine
Statue of the Holy Trinity

tanks was running for many decades to follow, and the energy cumulated in the basins was also used to run mills in the town.

In the 18th century, Banská Štiavnica was the biggest centre of extraction of bullion in the whole monarchy. Turkish threats were by that time averted for good, religious tensions calmed down, struggles between the Hungarian aristocracy and the royal court ceased to exist, and the long-lasting dispute between the mining towns and the public treasury was also settled. All of these were positively reflected in the town's economic and cultural development.

Empress Maria Theresé decided to establish the Mining Academy in Banská Štiavnica, being the first mining academy (meaning 'university' in today's terms) in Europe.

The heart of the town is Trinity Square, historically the most valuable site in Banská Štiavnica. In the 15th century the square was divided into two parts by building the Church of St. Catherine, which resulted in the emergence of two smaller squares, simply referred to as 'the upper' and 'the lower'.

The square is dominated by the massive Plague Column, which was built in the middle of it, following the plague epidemics of 1711. A number of burgher houses lining the square are also impressive.

What's interesting about these houses is the fact that, in the ground beneath them, they still hide corridors leading to old mining adits. These houses also were venues for interesting and historical events, and home to some interesting people.

For example, the Pischle House used to be home to Mária Pischlová, muse of the famous poet Andrej Sládkovič, inspiring him to write the most beautiful love poem in Slovak literature, *Marína*. Another is the richly decorated Fritz House, which used to be the seat of Mining Academy's Rector's Office, and also included a library and study hall. The Hallenbach House was originally the seat of Court of Mines and later of Mining Academy. Today, it houses the exposition installed by the Slovak Museum of Mining.

Architectonic highlights of the town are definitely the sacral sights on the Scharfenberg Hill. The complex includes three chapels, two churches and a cross with a stone sculpture of Our Lady of Seven Sorrows.

Speaking of sacral sights, the Calvary shouldn't be omitted, the top of which gives you a lovely view of the town and its surroundings.

For perceptive visitors, Banská Štiavnica is an open book of architecture, history and ecology.

BREZNO

Cultural Centre of the Upper Hron Area

Amid Brezno's square we find a building of an Evangelical parish, where the remarkable Slovak poet Ján Chalupka used to live. The building is at the same time the birthplace of another poet and cultural awakener Karol Kuzmány, and writer Martin Rázus spent a few years of his life here, too. This is not a coincidence, because the town of Brezno – as well as the whole Upper Hron area – was a centre of Slovak intellectuals in late the 19th and early 20th century. It was nothing unusual to meet poets, writers and painters here, as many of them lived, worked or frequented the town. Even famous Czech writer Božena Němcová often visited Brezno and its neighbourhood to collect folk tales and motifs for her stories. The breathtakingly splendid nature as well as the warm-hearted and fair-minded people

living here enchanted the fairytale collector Němcová. Brezno has grown from being a small Upper-Hron mining settlement, and over the centuries it had to struggle for its existence. Situated on an important trade route that led along the Hron River, Brezno used to administratively encompass a relatively extensive area reaching from the borders of the Malohont area on the south to the hills of Low Tatras on the north. At the same time, however, the town was wedged between two castle domains – Muráň and Ľupča – which often caused much historical tur-

bulence. Brezno, shortly after its emergence, suffered not only from armed conflicts, but also from the intrigues hatched by the Dóczys. They owned the castle in Ľupča, and at first they wanted to annex this prosperous town to their domain. When they failed to do so, they raided it on April 30, 1517, burnt it down, and killed many people here. King Ferdinand I gave Brezno a helping hand, bringing back town privileges to it (Brezno was for the first time granted privileges in 1380, but these were taken away from it meanwhile) along with exempting it from all taxes and other financial burdens. Despite all these advantages, the entire 15th century was a riotous period in the town. A slight calm came in the 16th century – when the steel factory began to be built in the nearby village of Hronec, later one of the biggest and most modern steelworks in the whole Hungarian Empire. In addition, the lands around Brezno were supplying the whole Banská Bystrica region with wood, which attracted many people to come here – mainly woodcutters and coal miners. In 1655 Brezno was promoted to a free royal town. Later, the iron and steel industry was developing in the town, and in modern times the engineering industry (chiefly bridge building and production of cranes) became the main industrial branch in Brezno.

A witness to the colourful history of the town is the square with several valuable sights, including the Town Hall built in 1770. The building has late-Baroque features, and is also decorated with the Brezno coat of arms. In the beginning of the 19th century, there was a tavern in the basement and the balcony used to be the venue for many important political events and speeches. Today the building houses the Horehronské Museum, where you can see a technical rarity – a horse-driven wringer.

Important milestones in the town's history
1241 – a devastating inroad by Tatars
1265 – the first written account of Brezno – in the document issued by King Belo IV
1380 – Brezno was granted town privileges
1517 – town was burnt down
1650 – King Ferdinand III promoted Brezno to a royal town
1779 – an extensive fire devastated the town
1895 – railway was built in Brezno
1946 – bridge building works founded

Famous personalities
Izák Caban (1659 – 1662), philosopher, teacher
Ján Simonides (1667 – 1673), writer
Ján Chalupka (1791 – 1871), poet
Karol Kuzmány (1806 – 1866), poet, first vice-chairman of Matica Slovenská
Gustáv Zechenter-Laskomerský (1824 – 1908), writer
Adolf Peter Záturecký (1837 – 1904), publicist,
Martin Rázus (1888 – 1937), writer
Ján Pohronský (1908 – 1995), writer

Places and sights worth visiting
Church of the Assumption
Church of the St. Cross
Evangelical church
Jewish synagogue
Municipal tower
Piarist Monastery and Chapel
Town Hall

◄ Façade of the birthplace of Karol Kuzmány

▲ The square is embellished by Municipal Tower, built in 1830..

▼ Horehronské Museum

BYTČA

Renaissance Gem

▲ Chateau in Bytča – Renaissance gem in Slovakia

▼ The chateau, being one of a few, maintained its original look.

Ruined Strečno Castle, which towers upon a limestone cliff on the left bank of the Váh River, hides secrets. Originally a fortress to collect tolls, built in the early 14th century, later turned into a royal castle. Several aristocrats owned it, and following the failed Wesselényi Uprising in 1698 Emperor Leopold I had it destroyed. Nowadays, Strečno is a popular tourist destination. Standing on the castle rocks, we can get a nice view of the surrounding countryside.

Beneath the cliff with the castle, the Váh River flows around a drab forested hill called Domašín, creating a river relief called Domašín Meander, unique in the Western Carpathians. Here we can find the notorious Margita and Besná cliffs, of which rafters used to be afraid because of several untimely deaths.

In the Váh valley, there lies the town of Bytča, dating as far back as 1234 - then a serf settlement belonging to the Nitra bishopric. It gradually became a little franklin (between a village and a town) and a centre of the local feudal domain. Given that it was controlled by rich people, construction ensued of a lovely Renaissance manor house, which remains Bytča's real architectonic gem. Under the aegis of the Thurzos family an area filled with various buildings sprouted up later on in the 16th century. They had an impressive manor house (a smaller chateau, so to say) built here that was designed to be a representative seat of the high state officer, which Thurzo was. The chateau was designed and built by an Italian master, Kilian of Milan. The massive building, with a central yard and arcades, has rounded bastions on its corners, and the walls of arcades facing the yard are decorated by wall paintings featuring various dukes and princes. Part of the chateau is the so-called Wedding Palace with rich sgraffito and decorative stonecut-

ting that was originally meant as a place for feasting and dance parties. The manor complex had to be rebuilt several times, with the first major restorations between 1605 and 1612, following a devastating revenge attack by catchpoles, who had failed to collect money from the owners. After the male branch of the Thurzos died off in 1621, the property was taken over by the Esterházys. They owned Bytča until the mid-19th century until, in 1862, the Poppers bought the manor with an eye to turning it into a source of future income. The family carried out further restorations, including rebuilding it into a block of flats, plus adjusting the Wedding Palace to become a seat of the district court. Notwithstanding all these reconstructions, Bytča's chateau hasn't lost any of its beauty and is now among the most impressive Renaissance sights in Slovakia from an architectural perspective. Among other interesting buildings that the town offers are: Gothic All Saints' Church adorning the square, smaller St. Barbara's Church at the municipal cemetery, Jewish synagogue and burgher houses on the square.

The surroundings of the town are attractive for tourists, too, as Bytča represents the start-off point for trips to the nearby mountains: Strážovské Mountains and Javorníky (Maple Mountains). Not far away, we can find a beautiful natural spot – often described as 'rocky town' – Súľovské Rocks. Here, nature carved out an impressive scene, featuring rocky towers, stilts, portholes and gates, all separated by deep clefts, valleys and gorges created without the help of waters and streams. The most beautiful creations here include the so-called Rocky Mushroom and 13-metre high Gothic Gate. The richest cluster of orchids in Slovakia, a waterfall and a castle in ruins (Súľovský Castle) also complement these natural treasures.

Important milestones in the town's history
1234 – Bytča became the property of the Nitra bishopric
1605 – the town was ravaged and burnt by catchpoles
1611 – the town witnessed the trial concerning auxiliaries of 'Bloody Countess' Elisabeth Bathory
1629 – the town was taken over by Mikuláš (Nicholas) Esterházy
1708 – Bytča was captured by Imperial army
1761 – the town suffered from an extensive fire
1858 – an earthquake stroke the town
1868 – Bytča and its manor bought by Leopold Popper

Famous personalities
Eliaš Láni (1575 – 1618), writer
Alexander Lombardini (1851 – 1897), historian
Sidónia Sakalová (1876 – 1948), writer
Milan Alexander Getting (1878 – 1951), journalist
Jozef Tiso (1887 – 1947), politician
Alojz Chura (1899 – 1979), doctor
Ivan Minárik, (1909 – 1967), writer
Ján Červeňanský (1905 – 1977), doctor

Places and sights worth visiting
All Saints' Church
Bytča's Chateau (manor house)
St. Barbara's Church
Synagogue
Wedding Palace

DOLNÝ KUBÍN

The Poetic Town

It's not exactly known in which house the young poet was staying when he came to the town of Dolný Kubín for the first time. But as soon as he finished his studies, he began to dwell in a house on the town's main square, opposite the library, where the poet's museum stands today. On the house there's a memorial plate installed, reading that Pavol Országh Hviezdoslav lived and worked here from 1900 to 1921, which was when he died.

This means that it was Dolný Kubín where most of his poetic works were written – in Slovak, which was largely unheard in that era of Hungarian dominance. Nowadays, his works represent the nation's best poetry and rank among the major works of the period in terms of European literature. The life and works of Hviezdoslav are commemorated by

his larger-than-life statue in front of Dolný Kubín's Museum building. Well-known Slovak sculptor Fraňo Štefunek, who also created the tombstone on the poet's grave, produced the statue.

Many literary personalities worked in Dolný Kubín, and the town has a long literary tradition. Annually, recitals by readers from all over Slovakia are featured in the Hviezdoslavov Kubín ('Hviezdoslav's Kubín') competition.

The area of Orava resembles a forgotten land, completely encircled by high peaks of the Western Tatras. In other words, it's a natural basin as if made for a rough but peaceful life. Mountain passes always crossed the mountains, providing natural protection for the basin. This seemingly idyllic land was a busy trade-and-military route.

Important milestones of the town's history
1325 – first written record of Dolný Kubin
1370 – Orava Castle became the seat of the domain
1556 – Orava Castle became a property of the Thurzos
1632 – Dolný Kubín was promoted from village to town

1683 – Dolný Kubin became the administrative centre of the Orava domain
1800 – Orava Castle was hit by fire
1834 – Dolný Kubín was hit by an extensive fire

Famous personalities
Janko Matuška (1821 – 1877), writer
Pavol Országh Hviezdoslav (1849 – 1921), poet
Pavol Bujnák (1882 – 1933), literary historian and critic
Ladislav Nádaši-Jégé (1886 – 1940), writer
Jozef Juraj Styk (1897 – 1965), politician
Theo H. Florin (1908 – 1973), poet, diplomat
Ján Johanides (1934), writer

Places and sights worth visiting
Church of St. Catherine
Florin's House
Memorial House of Pavol Országh Hviezdoslav
Museum of Pavol Országh Hviezdoslav
Orava Castle
Orava Gallery
Orava Museum

The town nestled in the heart of Orava – Dolný Kubín – was an important intersection, too. It emerged in the 14th century, and in 1683 became the seat of the Orava domain.

Its promising development was, however, disturbed by plundering Polish-Lithuanian armies, which were heading south to help Vienna in fighting Turks. Another disaster came in 1834 – the town was almost completely devastated by fire, and had to start anew.

The oldest preserved cultural and historical sight in Dolný Kubín is the Church of St. Catherine, built in the 14th century, but rebuilt five centuries later, following an extensive fire. Interesting item in the church's interior is the late-Gothic field altar.

The real pride of the town is its square, lined with Renaissance and Baroque burgher houses. The dominant one is the former Regional House, the façade of which is decorated by Orava's regional coat of arms from the 18th century.

Today the house is used by the Orava Gallery, which runs a permanent exposition of folk art, and installs various modern-art expositions here.

In the upper part of the square you can visit the Museum of Pavol Országh Hviezdoslav, which neighbours the Evangelical church, built between 1893 and 1894 in the place of a former 'tolerance' church that was destroyed by fire.

Those who visit Dolný Kubín surely won't pass up the chance to see Orava Castle, proudly towering on the rocky cliff above the village of Oravský Podzámok.

The castle was built in the place of former fortified fortress after the Tatar raids, in the times of northern Slovakia being settled.

It had many owners in the past, but its greatest glory dates between 1556 and 1626, when the aristocratic Thurzos family owned it.

They had the then-vacant and statically disturbed upper parts of the castle restored, and residential premises were moved mainly to the central and lower parts of the castle, where they also had their palace and a new chapel annexed.

In 1800 the castle was burnt out, and only after partial restoration works (carried out in 1868) one of first museums in Slovakia was installed here.

In the oldest part of the castle, you can visit an archaeological exposition documenting the oldest population of Orava region.

An exposition of natural sciences is situated on the ground floor, presenting fauna and flora of Roháče Mountains (part of the Western Tatras), the Orava Dam and the Orava Basin. The first floor houses the ethnographical exposition, which presents folk labour and the way of life in Orava's villages.

If you want to check your courage and nerves, you should go on a night tour around the castle, which is available during summer season only.

KREMNICA

The Town of Gold

The town of gold – this is the attribute that Kremnica gained in course of the 14th century, when this small town produced the highest amount of gold in the whole Hungarian Empire. In its blaze of glory, the town was enjoying the increased interest of rulers, who were trying to conquer it and control it for one simple reason: they wanted to possess its rich goldmines. A legend has it that Kremnica was founded based on a decision by a king, who, when attending a hunt in the mountains here, shot a partridge. When he had it served he found gold grains in the bird and commanded a search for gold to commence in Kremnica.

It is assumed that gold had already begun to be mined in Kremnica in the 10th century, but the real heyday period for the town was the 14th century. King Charles Robert of Anjou granted it with town privileges at that time, and later a mint was established producing gold and silver coins. Initially, famous Czech minters from Kutná Hora were employed here to introduce their know-how. Kremnica later started to mint Hungarian groschen, which were then followed by golden florins, known as Kremnica ducats. In the 16th century Kremnica's mint launched production of medals which still continues. Today, coins for different countries of the world are minted here, including commemorative coins.

Among the town's most significant highlights is Kremnica Castle, which had to be restored several times over the course of centuries, and which is the oldest castle in central Slovakia's mining area. Its architectonic structure was influenced by the fact that it was meant to protect the wealth produced by the local mint. Originally, it was a royal fortress where incomes from gold mining were

Important milestones in the town's history
1328 – Kremnica was granted town privileges
1560 – an extensive fire devastated the castle and one third of the town

Famous personalities
Ján Kollár (1793 – 1852), poet
Gustáv Zechenter-Laskomerský (1824 – 1908), writer
Pavol Križko (1841 – 1902), historian
Ján Levoslav Bella (1843 – 1936), composer
Michal Matunák (1866 – 1932), historian
Jaroslav Augusta (1878 – 1970), painter
Gejza Angyalov (1888 – 1956), painter
Jozef Ciger Hronský (1896 – 1960), writer
Peter Michalica (1945), violin virtuoso

Places and sights worth visiting
Church of St. Catherine
Church of St. John the Baptist
Goldmines
Kremnica's Castle
Museum of Coins and Medals
Roman-Catholic Franciscan church and monastery
Town Hall
Trinity Column

▲ A florin minted in Kremnica

▼ Kremnica Castle is the oldest castle in central Slovakia's mining area.

kept, as well as a 'safe' for coins minted in the royal mint, and that's why it differs from other feudal seats.

The oldest building of the castle area is Charnel House of St. Andrew, dating as far back as the 13th century. In the past, the charnel house was part of an erstwhile cemetery, which used to lie around St. Michael's Church. The skyline of the town is characterised today by a church with a Renaissance balcony. Architect Ferenc Storno, who was responsible for the overall neo-Gothic restoration of the area, designed its pitched roof in 1884. Storno also left his trace on the restoration of the church's interior. Several changes resulted in that only a part of an old mobiliari and a late-Gothic sculpture of Madonna survived. Both objects were brought here from the non-existing church, which used to stand on the town's square until the 19th century. The castle's buildings often suffered from fires in the past, which always required considerable financial resources to be used for restorations. However, the biggest catastrophe for the town was a depression in gold mining, which resulted in the town experiencing a period of decline.

An imposing adornment of Kremnica's square is a monumental Baroque-styled Trinity Column erected between 1765 and 1772 to commemorate the victims of plague epidemics that struck the town and almost wiped out its population in 1710. Rich sculptural decoration of the column is the work of famous sculptor Dionysius Stanetti. The Franciscan church with monastery, built during a massive anti-Reformation campaign led by ruling Hapsburgs, is also worth seeing. Very interesting is the building of local mint, which used to be specially walled and had its own armoury kept here. Tourists interested in becoming more familiar with the history of coin-minting and the production of medals in Kremnica should definitely visit the Museum of Coins and Medals, which is situated in one of the burgher houses on the square. The town also offers another unique museum – a permanent exhibition devoted to the history of skiing. In fact, Kremnica is the town where this white sport was born in Slovakia and many ski races are held on the slopes in the vicinity even today.

The whole area of Kremnica Castle was renewed in the 1990s. A robust organ, said to be one of the finest musical instruments in Slovakia, was installed in the interior of the Church of St. Catherine.

When talking about Kremnica, we mustn't omit its beautiful surroundings, represented by Kremnické Mountains. And there's something else that's special about this place: it's the spot assumed to be the symbolical centre of Europe. So, if you wish to come and stand in the centre of the old continent, you should go and look for a big rock-shaped memorial located at the walls of the Church of St. John the Baptist, which stands in the vicinity of the village of Kremnické Bane.

▲ Interior of the Church of St. Catherine

◄ One of the finest organs in Slovakia is installed inside the Church of St. Catherine.

▶ Sculpture of a man in the Church of St. Catherine

LIPTOVSKÝ MIKULÁŠ

Jánošík's Town

There's probably no other way to starting talking about Liptovský Mikuláš, the heart of the Liptov area, but to tell a story about Juraj Jánošík - the Slovak Robin Hood. This most famous bandit in the whole Austrian-Hungarian Empire became a legend for Slovaks, as well as a rich vein for writers, poets, painters, filmmakers, playwrights and musicians. Stories of his life and heroism reverberate from generation to generation, seemingly never to vanish from the memory of the Slovak nation. And today, no one really cares about which of the legends are based on facts and which simple fiction.

The fact is that in 1677 Liptovský Mikuláš became the centre of Liptov region, and that Juraj Jánošík was sentenced to death by hanging in Regional House in 1713. The execution was carried out shortly after, and Jánošík was hung on a hook inserted into his left ribs.

Anyway, the history of Liptovský Mikuláš goes much further back than that. Archaeologists found objects dating back to the late Bronze Age in the area of today's town. In the borough called Ondrašová, they found twelve bronze objects, and these represent the greatest findings from the Bronze Age discovered in the Carpathian Basin so far. In addition, archaeologists discovered a burial ground (a churchyard) and the blueprints of an older chapel (dated before 1200) around the Church of St. Nicholas.

The town, which was given name after St. Nicholas - a spiritual patron of the Church of St. Nicholas, gained sets of town privileges in the 14th and the 15th centuries. Thanks to this it became a market centre and a legal centre of the Liptov area. The 16th century was a positive period for the town's craftsmen - many of craftsmen's guilds were doing well. In the 18th century, a relatively large Jewish community lived in the town. The Jews built two synagogues and their own school here.

The dominant sight of Liptovský Mikuláš is, naturally, the Church of St. Nicholas, which stands in the middle of the

Important milestones in the town's history
1286 – the first written record of Liptovský Mikuláš
1299 – the first written accounts of the Church of St. Nicholas

1424 – the town was granted town privileges by King Sigmund
between 1677 and 1928 – Liptovský Mikuláš was the centre of Liptov region
1713 – Juraj Jánošík's trial took place
1883 – an extensive fire hit the town

Famous personalities
Juraj Jánošík (1688 – 1713), folk hero
Gašpar Fejérpataky-Belopotocký (1794 – 1874), publisher
Jozef Božetech Klemens (1817 – 1883), painter
Janko Kráľ (1822 – 1876), poet
Jan Levoslav Bella (1843 – 1936), composer

Aurel Stodola (1859 – 1942), inventor
Emil Stodola (1862 – 1945), politician
Kornel Stodola (1866 – 1946), economist
Miloš Ruppeldt (1881 – 1943), musician
Peter Július Kern (1881 – 1963), painter
Janko Alexy (1884 – 1970), painter
Martin Rázus (1888 – 1937), writer
Ivan Stodola (1888 – 1977), writer
Koloman Sokol (1902 – 2003), painter
Daniel Okáli (1903 – 1987), writer
Mária Rázusová-Martáková (1905 – 1964), writer
Anton Miroslav Húska (1905 – 1975), ethnographer
Ladislav Hanus (1907 – 1994), cultural theoretician

square. The first written account related to it comes from 1299. The oldest part of the church is the sacristy with Romanesque blueprints, which used to be a separate site in the past. In the middle of the 15th century a tower was built to extend the church and the whole sight was given a late-Gothic make-up.

Just for the record: in the past, the church was normally in the hands of Catholics, but it was Evangelists who ran it for the entire 17th century. The church was given Baroque look in the 18th century, and later – between 1940 and 1943 – the whole site underwent its most significant restoration. This meant that the church regained its original Gothic look, and side chapels were added to it, including new windowpanes (projects designed by Liptovský Mikuláš-born artists Janko Alexy, Fero Kráľ and Ján Želibský).

On the south side of the square, you can see three individual extra-lifesize statues made of sandstone. The Statue of St. Nicholas (patron of the town), the Statue of Janko Kráľ (one of the best Slovak poets), and the Statue of Gašpar Fejérpataky-Belopotocký (a well-known publisher) were installed here in 1948.

The highlight of the opposite side of the square is the Regional House, a late-Baroque building from 1793. Before the building went up, the regional authority was seated in the Illésházy Curia. Today it houses the Museum of Janko Kráľ, a famous poet who was born in Liptovský Mikuláš. Other famous natives haven't been forgotten, either. One example is the Gallery of Peter Michal Bohúň, who was a world-famous Slovak painter. The gallery was established in 1955 and, besides Bohúň's works, it offers Slovakia's artistic works dated between the 15th and the 18th century, plus works by Slovak painters and sculptors of the 19th and the 20th century.

Nearby stands a former seat of the richest family that ever lived in Liptovský Mikuláš – the Pongrác Curia, built in Gothic spirit and today houses the Centre of Koloman Sokol, a worldwide-acclaimed painter and graphic artist. Also a remarkable cultural sight is the building called Čierny orol ('Black Eagle'), formerly a tavern, in which all the important cultural events in the town took place. In present times, the building is used by the Liptovské Museum to install exhibitions.

Gejza Bárdoš (1908 – 1961), doctor
Milan Pišút (1908 – 1984), literary scientist
Pavol Strauss (1912 – 1994), writer

Places and sights worth visiting
Church of St. Nicholas
Čierny orol ('Black Eagle') building
Evangelical church
Gallery of Peter Michal Bohúň
Museum of Janko Kráľ
Pongrác Curia
Regional House

LUČENEC

The Mirror of Novohrad Region

Villages, towns and countries become famous for various reasons. Sometimes the events that made them famous are positive, sometimes negative. The centre of Novohrad region – the town of Lučenec – became most famous probably because of the Battle of Lučenec. It involved the revolutionary Brethren Movement and its 'divine warriors'. The Hussite tradition has an important place in Slovak and Czech histories, and is thus naturally linked to local histories of many of Slovakia's towns and villages.

However, Lučenec began to write its chronicle much earlier than in 1451, when the famous battle took place (in which the Hussites led by Ján Jiskra won over much stronger-in-size Hungarian troops led by János Hunyady). The most precious of many archaeological findings (testifying to this area being populated long ago) is a sword dating as far back as the late Bronze Age.

Historical sources related to the town show us much more valuable information, including, for example, a possibly apocryphal mention of building a chapel consecrated to Blessed Virgin Mary (allegedly 1128). It's contained in an account of German miners coming here at the command by King Ladislav IV. In 1275 he had purportedly sent them here to look for silver. Anyway, when it comes to solid accounts, the oldest known written document of Lučenec is the charter issued by King Belo IV in 1247, where Lučenec is referred to as Luchunch.

Lučenec witnessed a number of wars and other disasters in course of its history. In the second half of the 16th century it was controlled by Turks, who set the town on fire twice – during the uprisings of the Estates in the 17th century. As well as fires, the people of Lučenec suffered from frequent epidemics throughout the 18th century, and

Important milestones in the town's history
1247 – first written record of Lučenec

1442 – Lučenec was controlled by the Hussite armies
1451 – the Battle of Lučenec took place
1703 – an anti-Habsburg uprising (led by František Rákoczi),
       Lučenec citizens took part actively
1709 – epidemics of cholera hit the town
1819 – Lučenec hit by an extensive fire
1849 – imperial armies plundered the town and
       torched it

Famous personalities
Koloman Banšel (1850 – 1887), writer
Božena Slančíková-Timrava (1867 – 1951), writer

Places and sights worth visiting
Calvinist church
Evangelical church
Gallery of Novohrad
Golden Lane
Museum of Novohrad
Reduta
Roman Catholic church
Synagogue

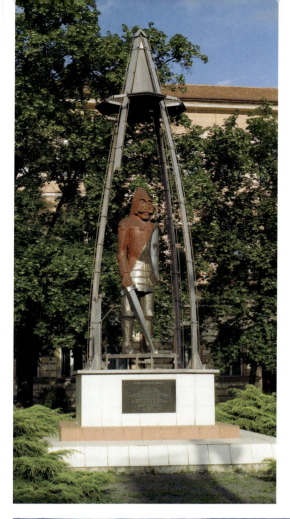

another shocking disaster was in 1849, a revolutionary year when military troops led by General P.C. Grabbe destroyed many buildings in the town.

Despite all these turbulent events, Lučenec always bounced back, especially economically, as the town was always an important centre of commerce and services in the area of Novohrad.

Unfortunately, frequent fires left traces on what has remained of historical sights in the town, so we can see only a limited number of sights today, documenting only Classicist and Secession architectonic styles. Among the best preserved sites belongs the Baroque-Classicist Roman Catholic church (from 1783), and a neo-Gothic Calvinist church (from 1853) which has a 64-metre tall tower with a rotating cock on its top. Of other sacral buildings in Lučenec, noticeable is also the Evangelical church (built in 1859), and the Secession-styled Jewish synagogue (from 1925) with distinctive Oriental features. When it comes to secular buildings, you can check out the Classicist building of Reduta, the Town Hall, and several Secession-styled houses from the end of the 19th century. An attractive site for tourists is the so-called Golden Lane with small shops, tearooms and cafes.

LEFT PAGE
▲ Roman Catholic church is one of the town's most interesting sacral sights.
◀ Reduta building, dated 1856, is now a centre of culture and commerce.
▶ Golden Lane features small shops and cafés

RIGHT PAGE
▲ 'Protector' of Novohrad area in Lučenec
▼ Lučenec's Pedagogical School and Calvinist church

MARTIN

Garden of Turiec

It's November 1, All Saint's Day, when people in droves visit cemeteries to pay honours to their loved one who have passed away. But there is a cemetery that's busy all year round – the National Cemetery in Martin, the last-resting place of more than three hundred famous people, including writers, artists, scientists and national awakeners from all corners of Slovakia. What was it that was attracting all these important personalities to come to this area? Was it all those splendid natural beauties in Turiec (hence the name 'Garden of Turiec'), or was it rather cultural values that were being born here?

The city's coat of arms best illustrates the history of Martin and the origin of its name. There's a golden-haired knight, Saint Martin, riding a horse, with his left hand holding his coat and his right hand holding a sword. Beneath, in front of him, a beggar kneels. According to historians and novelists, Martin of Tours was indeed a knight – a cavalryman of mercy. A legend has it that he helped the almost-frozen beggar by giving him half his coat, which he cut by his sword. This is how he saved the beggar's life.

That's what the legend reads, but the reality was different. According to archived documents, the area of Turiec was in the 12th century part of the Zobor abbacy. A document dated 1113 mentions some lands belonging to the abbacy, including Villa sancti Ypoliti (today Kláštor pod Znievom), Praun (today Slovenské Pravno), as well as a (now vanished) settlement called Wesscan. The lands of Lower Turiec were controlled by Sklabinský Castle and its owners. The castle, so famous in those times and so proudly towering over the nearby village of Sklabiňa, eventually

Famous personalities
Ján Kalinčiak (1822 – 1871), writer
Andrej Kmeť (1841 – 1908), man of science
Svetozár Hurban Vajanský (1847 – 1919), writer, national awakener
Pavol Országh-Hviezdoslav (1849 – 1921), poet
Jozef Škultéty (1853 – 1948), literary scientist
Elena Maróthy-Šoltésová (1855 – 1939), writer
Janko Jesenský (1874 – 1945), writer
Milan Thomka-Mitrovský (1875 – 1943), painter
Martin Benka (1888 – 1971), painter
Štefan Krčméry (1892 – 1955), writer

fell into ruins. In the 13th century, it was a royal castle and a seat of Turiec region. But fate wasn't kind to it. In 1436 it was burnt out, and although restored later, it was hit by another extensive fire in the end of the 16th century, which resulted in the castle being lost forever. Thanks to the romantic nature of Veľká Fatra Mountains, the ruins of the castle are covered by greenery for most of the year, so that the former walls can peacefully contemplate their faded glory.

The first indisputable written record of Martin, dating as far back as 1284, concerns the deed of donation issued by Hungarian King Ladislav IV. Martin was in 1340 granted town privileges by King Charles Robert. Promoting Martin to a town meant much greater economic opportunities and social advancement for its citizens, but these happy days were interrupted by the Hussite inroads into the basin of Turiec. The greatest damage was done by the Hussites when they were leaving the town, when they almost completely ravaged Martin and the neighbouring towns and villages. The chronicles available tell us about even more disasters that hit the region. From July 5, 1443, there's an account of such a strong earthquake that 'even towers were brought down'. In autumn of 1452, Martin was hit by the plague.

The town had to wait a few centuries to see the real development boom. The attention of the whole nation was paid to it only after the revolutionary year (1848), when it became the heart of the rising Slovak national, cultural and political movement. Martin was inscribed in Slovakia's history especially in June 1861, when it hosted a pan-national 'memorandum gathering' in front of the Evangelical church. At the gathering, claims of nationhood for Slovakia (it wasn't recognised as such within the Hungarian Empire), as well as claims for the fundamental rights of the nation, were formulated and articulated. The most important outcome of the Memorandum of the Slovak Nation was the establishment of Matica Slovenská (in 1863), an institution that then represented the only scientific, literary, artistic, edifying, political and social centre of Slovaks. Today it functions as the nation's cultural heritage organisation. Also, other institutions of national importance which had a similarly important role were born in Martin: a book-printing organisation, book-trade and publishers' organisation, Slovak women's league (called Živena), and others. Attempts to organise cultural and scientific life of Slovaks were in 1875 disrupted, and Matica Slovenská was shut down. Several personalities were later to successfully lobby for its re-launch (which took place in 1919), and notable among was Andrej Kmeť. A tireless organiser for science and research, Kmeť made a great contribution to building the first representative site of the Slovak Museum in Martin, and granted it most of his personal collection of books and his library. For example, his herbarium is the singularly important in Europe, as it includes 72,000 herbs. Besides this, he was also a passionate collector of precious archaeological, ethnological and folklore writings.

In addition, in terms of Slovakia's cultural life, Martin went down in history also as a theatre town (city), with many famous Slovak actors performing here.

LEFT PAGE
▲ Statutes of Matica Slovenská – historical document
◄ Matica Slovenská
► Turčianska Gallery is situated inside the former Regional House.

RIGHT PAGE
◄ Matica Slovenská building
► Jozef Škultéty's grave at the National Cemetery
▼ Precious Gothic fresco inside St. Martin's Church

Janko Alexy (1894 – 1970), painter
Karol Plicka (1894 – 1987), photographer, folklorist
Jozef Ciger-Hronský (1896 – 1960), writer
Miloš Bazovský (1899 – 1968), painter
Oľga Országhová-Borodáčová (1899 – 1986), actress
Hana Meličková (1900 – 1978), actress
Ľudovít Fulla (1902 – 1980), painter
Ján Marták (1903 – 1982), literary historian
Mária Rázusová-Martáková (1905 – 1964), writer
Zora Jesenská (1909 – 1972), translator
Svetozár Stračina (1940 – 1996), composer

Places and sights worth visiting
Ethnographical Museum
Evangelical church
Museum of Martin Benka
Museum of Slovak Village
National Cemetery
National House
National Library
Regional House (Turčianska Gallery)
Slovak National Museum of Literature
St. Martin's Church

NOVÁ BAŇA

The Land of Precious Metals

There are many mining towns in Slovakia that used to profit from extracting precious metals in the past.

One of them is Nová Baňa, which was for centuries hidden in the shadow of nearby and much more famous town of Banská Štiavnica. The facts have it clear – Nová Baňa, perhaps even in the times of Roman Empire, was an important centre of commerce. Many archaeological findings of coins from that period bear witness to this.

The trade route leading along the Hron River was later protected by a fortified settlement looking out over the entire area. The massive castle, standing on a hill near what's now Nová Baňa, was encircled by a robust mound and moat, which can be seen on the hill's horizon even today.

It was mainly the local deposits of precious metals that attracted the first settlers. The chronicle of Nová Baňa dates back to 1337, from when the first written record of a settlement called Seunich comes. The local deposits of gold were rich then, which attracted more and more people.

The settlers were building mills to crush the ores, and the settlement soon started

Important milestones in the town's history
1337 – oldest known written record of a settlement called Seunich
1345 – Nová Baňa was granted privileges of a free royal mining town
1348 – first sealed document was issued for the town

1723 – gold-mining company was established in Nová Baňa
1887 – local mines were shut down

Famous personalities
Ervin Holéczy (1897 – 1977), writer
František Švantner (1912 – 1950), writer

Places and sights worth visiting
Chapel of Our Lady in the village of Kohútovo
Church of the Saint Cross
Church of the Virgin Mary
Pohronské Museum

to turn into a small town. In 1345 Nová Baňa gained the status of a free royal mining town, and later was given the right to hold markets and the right of sword (to carry out executions). This is all recorded in historical documents, reading which we learn that the biggest boom in the town came in the second half of the 14th century, when it was ranked among seven mining towns of Upper Hungary.

However, the glory didn't last long, as the town was drawn in to the internal unrest of Hungarian Empire. It was unable to resist Turkish invasions and avoid an uprising of the Estates, plus it was hit by a wave of plague epidemics that almost exterminated the town's population in the 17th century.

Even mining activities were declining due to technical problems concerning downstream water flooding the mines. To save the flooded mines, a unique pumping device (constructed by an English engineer Isaac Potter in 1722) was used. It was the first steam engine practically used in Europe.

The device indeed helped the mines. In 1723, a gold-mining company was established in Nová Baňa, which after some success and a lot of bad luck saw the mines eventually shut down in 1887.

Thanks to economic prosperity that gold mining brought in the past, we can see a number of valuable historical sights. The dominant one is the Town Hall, which was built in 1335 as a royal house (*domus regiae*). According to a directive issued by Hungarian King Charles Robert, such a house had to stand in every town around the country. As of the 18th century the building was used as the Town Hall, and after later being restored it became a seat of the Pohronské Museum.

In the past the town was living an active spiritual life. The Church of St. Elisabeth was built here already in 1391. The locals usually call it *Špitálsky kostolík* ('Hospital Church'), as it used to be part of a no-longer existing hospital. The church was in 1664 captured by Turks, and later it belonged to Protestants.

Following the restoration in 1893, the church took on its current look. Inside the church, you can see a painting that features a scene of the Good Shepherd and St. Elisabeth.

The forgotten but rich past of this mining town is well illustrated by the valuable decorations of the Church of the Virgin Mary, which was originally built in Gothic style.

Rugged, rolling hills above the town surround the Church of the Saint Cross,

which can be accessed by walking up on a path lined by chapels symbolising the Stations of the Cross.

In the nearby village of Kohútovo stands a small holy shrine (dating back to 1863) – the Chapel of the Virgin Mary with a stone statue of Immaculata, which is completely surrounded by trees.

Southwards from Nová Baňa, above the village of Hronský Beňadik, we can spot a massive Benedictine monastery, which is one of the oldest and most valuable architectonic sites in Slovakia.

It was founded in 1075 based on a decision of King Gejza II, who wanted to colonise this thinly-populated valley of the Hron River and to support the proselytisation of the area. The oldest part of the monastery was a Roman basilica, rebuilt in Gothic style between 1346 and 1375.

POVAŽSKÁ BYSTRICA

Beautiful Skyline of Castle in Ruins upon the Váh River

Panorama of the country along the Váh River is made up by a number of castles in ruins. More than anywhere else in Slovakia, they remind us of the almost forgotten past, and with their dignity they make us stop here for a while as we're passing. On a precipitous hill situated on the right bank of the Váh River, we can see the skyline of the Považský Castle in ruins, once a seat of marauding knights who represented a threat in this corner of Slovakia in the past.

Favourable climate of this small basin, rounded by a ring of mountains, as well as the fertile ground and an advantageous location on an important trade route leading along the Váh – all these circumstances attracted people to move here even in ancient times. Shards of ceramics, dating back to the Baden culture (late Stone Age, some 4,500 years ago), represent the oldest found artefacts that provide evidence of today's Považská Bystrica being populated. The first written record of the town comes from 1316, the very next from 1330. The history of the town is closely connected with the history of Považský Castle, which is al-

Important milestones in the town's history
1316 – the first written record of Považská Bystrica
1432 – Hussites set the town on fire
1435 – Považská Bystrica was granted town privileges
1458 – the town was donated to Ladislav Podmanický
1506 – installation of the town's statute

1656 – the town was granted set of new privileges, which
      extended its rights
1886 – Považská Bystrica lost the status of a town
1914 – Považská Bystrica was promoted to a large village
1946 – the town regained its municipal status

Famous personalities
Imrich Weiner-Kráľ (1901 – 1978), painter
Vladimir Miro (1910 – 1976), writer
Michal Lukniš (1916 – 1986), geographer

Places and sights worth visiting
Chateau in the village of Orlové
Považský Castle

▲ Originally Renaissance chateau from
early 17th century

▼ Romantic backwaters of the Váh River

ready mentioned in 1316, together with the name of Matúš Čák of Trenčín.

However, only a few documents on both the castle and the town itself have survived, because Hussites torched Považská Bystrica in 1432, destroying not only people's dwellings but also valuable documents. Thus, only documents dated later give us an account of the town's history. King Sigmund granted Považská Bystrica town privileges in 1435. In 1458, King Matthias Corvinius gave the town (together with another 16 villages) to Ladislav Podmanický, which kicked off a 100-year period of the Podmanickýs (a noble family) being in charge of the castle. When Ján Podmanický, Ladislav's son and later a mayor of Bratislava and captain of Bratislava Castle, inherited the demesne of what is now Považská Bystrica, he had a Gothic church built in the town. At the same time he became the church's premier private patron, which gave him the right to select clergymen if these were pre-approved by the Bishopric office. Besides this, he installed the statute of the town, in which some guilds and a public school are mentioned. Považská Bystrica was, except for Varín, the only town in Slovakia where Slovak was the language used exclusively by guild masters.

The situation in the town and in the castle changed when the last of the Podmanickýs – Ján and Rafael, ardent supporters of Hungarian King Ján Zápoľský – began to violently occupy and take charge of the properties of their enemies. Later, they requested that the king donate these domains to them. That's when they gained the tainted reputation of 'marauding knights'. With the death of Rafael in 1558, the family of Podmanickýs died off.

Then the domain went to the hands of a powerful and influential family – the Balaššs. Despite the unlucky historical period, which was typical of numerous uprisings of the Estates, rulers kept on granting new privileges to Považská Bystrica. The bestowing of these privileges made the town more and more prestigious and progressive compared to the surrounding towns and villages. Municipal events started to be more properly recorded in the chronicle in 1716. In it we learn, for example, that mayors of the town were elected on St. George's Day, while legal issues were dealt with by a notary (a lawyer), and economic affairs together with the town's properties were administrated by a reeve (whom people called 'gazda'). The town was also employing gamekeepers, shepherds and a harbinger.

The quite peaceful life of the town was disrupted by a series of natural disasters throughout the 19th century – floods, fires, epidemics and an earthquake. Historical documents have revealed that more than a hundred of people died during a flood in 1813, and that cholera carried off 135 people here in the summer of 1831. One part of the town burnt out in 1832 and the other in 1834, and a powerful earthquake hit the area of the castle in 1858.

In 1886, Považská Bystrica (being a serf town) lost its status of a town, but only until 1917 when the Trenčín regional congregation promoted it to become a large village. After WWII, it became a town, and since 1948 it has been a district town.

Apart from the castle in ruins, the cultural-historical highlight is a chateau in a nearby village of Orlové. On the hill in Považská Bystrica, we can visit St. Helen's Chapel, dated 1728.

▲ Epitaph from the church in Považská Bystrica

▼ Považský Castle – an quintessential part of the Váh River Basin

RAJEC

Healing Water Hot Springs

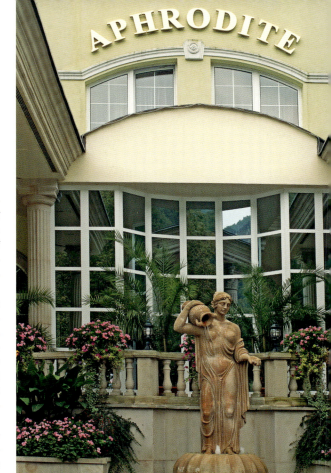

Some towns gradually grow and gain in importance, while others lose their status. With its importance and size, the town of Rajec in the second half of the 19th century used to be far ahead of Žilina, for example. Only slightly more than 6,000 people live here now and, frankly, Rajec is less well known than are its neighbours - the spa town of Rajecké Teplice and the village of Rajecká Lesná.

However, the history of Rajec started to be written as early as in 1193. Then it was just a settlement, but in the 14th century it was developing into a small town, or a larger village. In the 17th century, Rajec was granted a set of privileges (including the right to hold fairs and markets) and became a crafts centre. It was then that the town became famous for exporting its typical red leather - called 'rajčianka'

- all around the kingdom. The most valuable document related to the history of the town is the one issued by Empress Maria Theresé in 1749, which freed people of Rajec from paying tolls all around the empire, and which is now kept in the Municipal Museum.

The museum also has a furnished room inside, representing typical dwellings in Rajec from the beginning of the 20th century. The museum also houses a crafts workshop where making textiles, wicker, straw and products are authentically produced and presented exactly as they were in the past. Artistic representations of local masters are famous around the world.

One such master is Jozef Pekar, a carver from the nearby village of Rajecká Lesná who put together the well-known Slovak Bethlehem.

Important milestones in the town's history
1193 - first written record of Rajec (referred to as a settlement)
1376 - first written record of spa area in Rajecké Teplice

1749 - Empress Maria Theresé freed Rajec citizens from paying tolls anywhere in the Hungarian Empire
1937 - modern hotel facilities in the spa area in Rajecké Teplice were built

Famous personalities
Juraj Slota (1819 - 1882), teacher, editor
František Šujanský (1832 - 1907), collector of folk tales
Andrej Černiansky (1841 - 1923), editor
Cyril Gabriel Zaymus (1843 - 1894), teacher
Vojtech Kállay (1887 - 1956), regional governor
Andrej Rybárik (1897 - 1965), writer

Matúš Kavec (1898 - 1980), writer
Ferdinand Ďurčanský (1906 - 1974), politician
Margita Velehrachová-Matulayová (1909 - 1990), writer
Ján Kempný (1912 - 1997), politician
Rudolf Pribiš (1913 - 1984), sculptor

Places and sights worth visiting
Church of St. Ladislav in Rajec
Church of the Assumption in Rajecké Teplice
Municipal Museum in Rajec
Slovak Bethlehem in Rajecká Lesná
Spa area in Rajecké Teplice

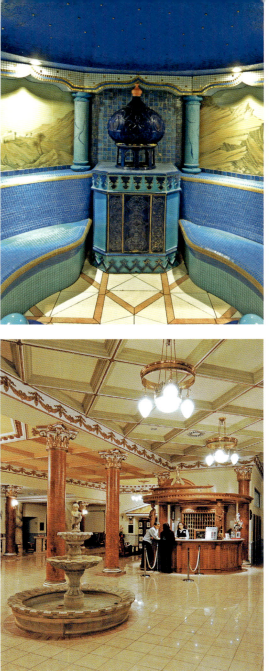

The Bethlehem, which took a painstaking 15 years to produce, is 8.5 metres long, 2.5 metres in width and 3 metres high; features 300 figures – half of them moving.

The village of Rajecká Lesná is nestled in the shadow of Kľak Mountain, down in Rajecká Valley. Roofs of local wooden houses stick out into narrow streets, as if looking for the path leading to the local medieval church with its Gothic statue of Virgin Mary the Queen. The village was called Frivald until 1948, and people have been coming here for centuries to enjoy the curative effects of the healing waters emanating from five springs.

Rajecké Teplice grew up next to the thermal springs, which are located in the vicinity of another village – Konská. The first written account of the town comes from 1376, being referred to as 'villa Topolcha'.

In the beginning of the 17th century the first spa house (including seven rooms for guests and a tavern) was built near the springs. Since then Rajecké Teplice have been developing as a spa resort. The greatest glory was witnessed here towards the end of the 18th century.

At that time there were three pools – one for aristocrats, one for bourgeoisie, and one for common people. The visiting rate of the spa resort increased even more after the railway along the Váh River was built, and its popularity was boosted by a visit from members of Vienna's imperial court in 1889.

Today, the spa area in Rajecké Teplice ranks among the best spa resorts in Slovakia and is visited mostly by people with rheumatic diseases and locomotion disorders, as well as various neuroses and occupational diseases.

One especially attractive spa house is called Aphrodité, which is done up in antique style.

LEFT PAGE
▲ Spa house Aphrodité
◄ Town Hall building dated 16ᵗʰ century stands amidst the square.
► Church of the Assumption

RIGHT PAGE
◄ An attractive spa house Aphrodité in Rajecké Teplice is done up in antique style.
► Carved Bethlehem in Rajecká Lesná

RIMAVSKÁ SOBOTA

A Witness to Remarkable Historical Events

Let's start our trip to Rimavská Sobota (which is the centre of historical Malohont, and the centre of former Gemer-Malohont administrative region) a little bit untraditionally - by visiting the Gemer-Malohont Museum. At first glance, the museum seems to be in no way special: just like many other regional ones in Slovakia it is oriented toward history, ethnography, arts and nature of the region. But when we take a look around more carefully, we find here a really unique exhibit - a mummified body of a woman. I. S. Munkácsi, a lawyer from Rimavská Sobota, donated the mummy to the museum having brought it from Egypt in 1910. The woman's name was Tasheritnetiakh, and she lived in the Egyptian town of Abusir-El-Melek sometime between 1087 and 664 BC, the period of dynasties 21-25. Interesting about her is that she died when she was over fifty, which was a rarity in those times, as the average length of life was forty in ancient Egypt. The mummified body is one of four such pieces kept in museum collections in Slovakia. The Gemer-Malohont Museum itself is a rarity, too - belonging among the oldest museums in Slovakia. Part of the museum is a historical cultural collection of more than 32,000 old books.

Precursor of the town lying on a fertile alluvial land on the banks of the Rimava River was a settlement from the 11th century, named after the first Hungarian King Stephen I - 'Villa Stephani'. Due to markets held in the town regularly on Saturdays, the settlement began to be called *Sobota* ('Saturday'), and the record from 1270 has it referred to as *Rymoa Zumbota*. Between 1441 and 1460 it was in the hands of Ján Jiskra of Brandýs (a Hussite leader), and thus witnessed several important historical events, such as the declaration of a truce between the Hussites and imperial representatives. However, the town also witnessed a number of catastro-

phes and natural disasters. In 1506 it was hit and destroyed by fire, and its fate was negatively affected by a series of Ottoman-Turkish occupations, too. Only towards the end of the 18th century Rimavská Sobota became a free town, and later the seat of Gemer-Malohont administrative region.

Nonetheless, also in the decades to come the town came to witness influential events of historical importance. To mention at least one of them, a famous Russian army-leader Mikhail Kutuzov –returning from the Battle of Austerlitz in 1805 - stayed overnight in Rimavská Sobota.

In the past, Rimavská Sobota was known especially for its commercial and craft-related activities, and thanks to its fertile soil also for farming, and the town is also known as an educational centre. A community of intellectuals was established here, significantly contributing to the development of cultural and social life of the whole region. History of the town remarkably influenced the town's architecture. Rimavská Sobota has a nicely trimmed square with historical buildings along the sides. The highlight of the square is right in its centre - the Classicist Roman Catholic Church of St. John, built between 1774 and 1790 where an old Gothic church used to stand. The old one belonged to Calvinists when the Reformation Movement was in control. After religious tensions taking place later, Empress Maria Theresé decided to bring it down in 1771, and the new - Catholic - sanctuary was built here instead. A little further from the square, you can see the Baroque-Classicist Evangelic church from between 1784

▲ Late-Romanesque Evangelical church in Rimavská Baňa

▼ Hotel Tatra on the square

Important milestones in the town's history

1270 – first written record of a settlement referred to as Rymoa Zumbota

between 1441 and 1460– town controlled by the Hussite armies led by Ján Jiskra
1506 – town was hit by fire
1805 – legendary Russian army-leader Kutuzov stayed overnight in the town
1831 – town was hit by cholera epidemics

Famous personalities
Štefan Ferenci (1792 – 1856), sculptor
Július Botto (1829 – 1881), historian
Jozef Škultéty (1853 – 1948), literary historian and writer
Terézia Vansová (1963 – 1868), writer

Ivan Krasko (1876 – 1958), poet
Tibor Kolbenheyer (1917 – 1993), geophysicist
Libuša Mináčová (1925 – 2005), writer

Places and sights worth visiting
Calvinist church
Evangelical church
Gemer-Malohont Museum
Observatory
Reduta
Regional House
Roman Catholic Church of St. John the Baptist

and 1790, built as a tolerance sanctuary and in 1808 restored in a historicising style. Calvinists built their new church in 1784, and extended it in the 19th century. There used to be a Jewish synagogue (built 1858) in the town, but it was later knocked down. Secular sights worth checking out include the Regional House (in the style of French Baroque), the building of former Town Hall (in Classicist style), and the Reduta building. Generally speaking, Rimavská Sobota was well known especially for its grammar school in the past. Several famous intellectuals (mostly artistic souls) studied here, including historian Július Botto, literary historian, linguist Jozef Škultéty, poet Ivan Krasko and the female writer Terézia Vansová.

▲ Classicist Roman Catholic Church of John the Baptist

▶ Interior of the Evangelical church in Rimavská Baňa.
Part of the fresco featuring Ladislavian legend
in the church in Rimavská Baňa

▼ The square also has the building of former Classicist Town Hall dated 1801.

RUŽOMBEROK

Rosy History Full of Thorns

Ružomberok, a district town situated in the Lower Liptov area, was in the past famous for growing roses and today it is well known for production of paper. In the place where the town's square is now, there used was once a hillock grown-over by bushes of wild roses. That's why it wasn't difficult to decide what name to give to the town – it was called Rosenberg ('Hill of Roses'). Later, Slovak form of the name – Ružomberok – was coined, and remained to date.

The town was founded on an important junction of European trade routes, which were leading from central Slovakia's mining towns to Poland, and from Košice through the Spiš area to Žilina, and from there to Silesia. Ružomberok's direct predecessor was a Slavic fortified village,

the first written account of which comes from 1233.

In 1318, when colonists (German miners) already populated the area, Ružomberok was granted the first set of town privileges, and these were later (in 1340) extended by another set given by King Charles Robert which freed Ružomberok from regional jurisdiction. The town's citizens were allowed to go fishing in the local river (called Revúca) and freely mine gold, silver and copper.

At that time, neighbouring villages Vlkolínec, Biely Potok, Černová and Ludrová belonged to the town as well. In 1390, King Sigmund gave the town to lords of Likava, which meant that Ružomberok became a province town for a certain period.

Important milestones of the town's history
1233 – first written record of a Slavic fortified village
1318 – first set of town privileges was granted to Ružomberok
1340 – new privileges were granted to the town
1390 – King Sigmund gave the town to lords of Likava
1725 – paper-mill was founded in Ružomberok

1868 – first of Slovakia's amateur theatre had its premiere performance
1912 – first cinema in Slovakia opens in Ružomberok
1912 – Liptov's Museum Society founded in the town
1993 – the village of Vlkolínec put on the UNESCO World Heritage List

Famous personalities
Matúš Dulla (1846 – 1926), politician
Andrej Hlinka (1864 – 1938), Catholic priest, publicist and politician
Dušan Makovický (1866 – 1921), doctor
Vavro Šrobár (1867 – 1950), politician
Fedor Houdek (1877 – 1953), politician, publicist
Vojtech Budinský-Krička (1903 – 1993), archaeologist

Jozef Felix (1913 – 1977), literary scientist
Ľudovít Fulla (1902 – 1980), painter

Places and sights worth visiting
Calvary
Chateau of St. Žofia
Church of St. Andrew
Church of the Holy Family
Church of the Saint Cross
Evangelical church
Gallery of Ľudovít Fulla
Liptovské Museum
Marian column
Mausoleum of Andrej Hlinka

Nevertheless, crafts were doing well; guilds and smaller manufactures were founded in the town. The well-known paper-mill was founded before 1720.

Let's stop for a while in a nearby village of Vlkolinec, because this little excursion outside the town is really worth the visit. Thanks to its remarkable folk architecture, Vlkolinec was included in UNESCO's list of World Heritage List in 1993. Today, the village is ranked among the most visited tourist destinations in Slovakia. The oldest building in the village is the rustic shingled bell-tower from 1770, around which wooden houses are nested. Another dominant sight in Vlkolinec is the wooden well, which used to be the only source of drinking water in the village.

The historical core of Ružomberok is a monumental reserve. The Andrej Hlinka Square has managed to keep its peculiar ambience, with its typical burgher houses from the 18th century.

The most valuable sacral sight in the town is the Gothic Church of St. Andrew (dated 14th century), in the vicinity of which a parish used to stand in the past. In the parish, Andrej Hlinka (a Catholic priest, publicist and politician) used to work. Eye-catchers on the square are also the Piarist monastery and the Church of the Saint Cross. Among the representative secular buildings are the neo-Baroque Town Hall, the Liptovské Museum, and also the Gallery of Ľudovít Fulla. It includes well-documented life work of this world-famous Slovak painter, graphic artist and illustrator. The Evangelical church, the Roman Catholic Church, and several secession buildings are worth checking out, too.

When leaving the town and heading towards the village of Ludrová, you can spot the Gothic Chateau of St. Žofia, originally a Gothic medieval site resembling a fortress, and a Marian column from 1858.

It wasn't until the 19th century, when a pulp-mill, a paper-mill, a textile factory, a cheese factory and a match factory were gradually founded, that industry developed dynamically.

In the early 20th century, Ružomberok was one of the most important centres of Slovakia's national life, though the town had been culturally active since the 17th century, and the first of Slovakia's amateur theatre had its premiere performance here in 1868.

As of 1912, the first cinema in Slovakia (called Apollo) opened. The same year, the brothers Artur and Július Kurtiovs established the Liptovské Museum. Visitors here have a unique chance to admire a hat which is said to have been worn by the famous Slovak bandit Juraj Jánošík, often called the Slovak Robin Hood.

LEFT PAGE
◀ Church of St. Andrew
▶ Main altar in the church

RIGHT PAGE
◀ Parish Office
▶ Statue of Andrej Hlinka
▼ Burgher houses on the square

SLOVENSKÁ ĽUPČA

Royal Dowry

An important route led through the valley along the Hron River in medieval times – Via Magna. The route also crossed through the village of Slovenská Ľupča, which first appeared in the existing written documents in 1250. In the 13th century, the village was even more often mentioned in the documents than others around. A particularity about the village is the way it was populated; as the population was divided into two parts – one was located around a medieval castle, while the other around a medieval monastery belonging to Franciscan monks.

The history of Ľupčiansky Castle also goes a long way back. The first record of the castle comes from 1306. The castle was situated in a splendid environment, amid forests full of wildlife, and that's presumably why it was enjoyed so much by many kings and lords. Anyway, its fate was mostly influenced by a series of weddings, as for many years it was a part of dowries for Hungarian queens. Eventually in 1620, it became the property of Széchys, and Hungarian Palatine George Wesselényi obtained it by marrying Maria Széchy. This fate was a godsend to the castle, because – despite the fact that Wesselényi (leader of one of the anti-Hapsburg uprisings) turned it into his noble seat – the castle's solid walls resisted the force of the Imperial army. The emperor actually did not focus many of his forces on this castle, unlike on the other castles around the country. Thanks to these lucky circumstances, Ľupčiansky Castle has survived in a very good condition until these days. What a pity that it's not open to the public!

Ľupča was later promoted to a town, although it was actually only a small one. During his visit to the castle in November 1340, Hungarian King Charles Robert gave it town privileges, which significantly pushed Ľupča forward, gradually becoming a thriving little town. However, this wasn't enough for town representatives in Ľupča, so they called on authorities to promote it to a royal town with relevant legal and economical privileges, including the right to elect vicars and mayors, as well as the right to hold fairs and markets. The small town wanted to compare to bigger towns, so it established a lyceum.

However, the Turkish invasions halted the successful development of the town, as these incursions represented the biggest threat for Slovaks in the 16th century. And once they had successfully resisted Turkish raids, there was another threat to come – the plague, which came in waves. In 1679 alone, more than seven hundred people died from this disease, so the memorial to the victims of plague was erected in the town – the Plague Column.

Anyway, life goes on and even terrible disasters gradually become past. So it was in Ľupča – the town was vibrant with the life of craftsmen during the 17th century. The most prosperous crafts here included coopers, shoemakers and cutlers. Also the first paper-mill was flourishing, producing paper until 1920. Later, some other successful crafts and industries arrived such as a flour mill, sawmill, brick factory and stone quarry. Slovenská Ľupča lost its town privileges in the second half of the 19th century, and so it became a village again. Business activities were not affected. Quite the opposite – furniture manufacture was established here, along with a bell foundry workshop, a chemical plant, and others.

Throughout the 20th century, the village went basically in line with the situation in Slovakia and elsewhere: it survived WWI, the Global Economic Depression, WWII, and so on. In 1953, construction works at the pharmaceutical factory (Biotika) began, thanks to which the village is still known.

Famous personalities
Samuel Reuss (1783 – 1852), historian
Daniel Gabriel Lichard (1812 – 1882), publisher, editor
Samuel Cambel (1856 – 1909), linguist
Emil Belluš (1899 – 1979), architect
Tibor Andrašovan (1917 – 2001), composer

Places and sights worth visiting
Building of former town hall
Corvinius's Linden (a protected tree)
Ľupčiansky Castle
Neo-Gothic Evangelical church
Plague Column
Roman-Catholic church

▲ Ľupčiansky Castle
▼ Gothic church in Slovenská Ľupča

TVRDOŠÍN

As Beautiful as a Painting

One of the best known Orava natives was the academic painter Mária Medvecká, whose artistic works were chiefly inspired by this breathtakingly beautiful area. The painter, born in the village of Medvedzie (now part of Tvrdošín) was gladly returning to her native land throughout her life. Today, there is the Gallery of Mária Medvecká in Tvrdošín, a permanent exposition installed by the Orava Gallery.

Tvrdošín was at first a toll-collecting station for the trade between Hungarian Empire and Polish Kingdom, through which mainly salt, lead and clothes were traded. Later, it was a fortress belonging to the Orava domain. Only in 1369 King Louis I the Great granted it with privileges of a royal town. Tvrdošín kept its privileges and rights throughout the centuries to come. In the 15th century the town was developing moderately, but in the 16th century it markedly declined. In the 17th century, a series of anti-Hapsburg uprisings and Jan Sobieski-led Polish-Lithuanian armies crossing this area in 1683 caused serious damage and loss. Tvrdošín began to improve gradually only in the 18th century, with people mainly engaged in farming and grazing cattle. Additional revenues were flowing from sawmill, fairs, markets, two mills, hop shop and crafts (chiefly drapery and later also raft making). Other crafts in the town were wood processing, tannery, dye house and a button-maker.

The sights in Tvrdošín include the late-Gothic wooden Church of All Saints, built at the local cemetery in the latter half of the 15th century, inside of which you can admire a set of valuable paintings. Once the church had a low Gothic altar from which only a wing with a painting of St. Peter and St. John the Baptist has survived. The central part of the altar originally contained a painting called 'Grieving over Christ' (15th century), which was in 1919 taken to a museum in Buda-pest, Hungary. Rebuilding and restoration works on the church were in 1993 awarded by a prestigious 'Europa Nostra' plate, and the church itself, as a national monument, was put on UNESCO's List of World Cultural Heritage. Other sights in Tvrdošín include the late-Baroque column from the end of the 18th century, the Baroque chapel from 1815, and local yeoman houses.

The town today also includes parts called Krásna Hôrka and Medvedzie, which used to be individual villages in the past. Krásna Hôrka, once a serf village under the Orava domain, attracts visitors thanks to its Baroque chapel, bell tower and Marian column. Medvedzie, which emerged in 1355 as a yeoman village, later belonged to the family of the Medveckýs. Valuable architectonic sites are represented here by Classicist curia from the late 18th and early 19th centuries.

▲ Altar in the wooden Church of All Saints
▶ Detail of the church's pulpit
▼ Gallery of Mária Medvecká

Important milestones in the town's history
1265 – first written record, found in a document issued by King Belo IV
1369 – Tvrdošín was granted town privileges
1683 – an anti-Hapsburg uprising

Famous personalities
Albert Škarvan (1869 – 1926), writer
Mária Medvecká (1914 – 1987), painter

Places and sights worth visiting
Church of All Saints
Church of the Holy Trinity
Gallery of Mária Medvecká

ZVOLEN

From Fort to Castle

King Louis the Great of Anjou had a royal castle built in the vicinity of Zvolen in the last third of the 14th century. It was projected according to Italian town castells; and since Gothic style was the most influential architectonic movement in those times, the castle was being built in this glamorous style – in order to make it a comfortable place for visitors and guests coming here for hunting. Comfort of the castle also included a lovely view from the rooms in its northern wing – a view of Zvolen's square. On the ground floor of Zvolen Castle we find a large hall with a stone rib vaulted ceiling lit up by narrow apertured windows. In this hall, towards the courtyard of the castle, we can admire seats that survived to date, on which aristocratic hunters used to sit around the table when celebrating their successes. However, the most monumental hall in the

castle is the Chivalric Hall, which occupies the whole wing of the first floor.

Like many other similar sites in Slovakia, Zvolen Castle was unable to avoid frequent restorations carried out by its owners. In 1548, it underwent a restoration in the spirit of Renaissance, including building up one floor and adding four corner towers with dormer windows. Later restorations did not largely influence the castle's look. What's especially worth checking out in the castle is the large hall in the west wing, where you can admire lovely painted ceiling dating back to the 18th century, including portraits of Roman emperors and Hapsburg rulers. Slovak National Gallery uses rooms in the castle to expose the national collection of Gothic and modern art, and the castle's courtyard is every summer a lively place where theatre performances organised by the Theatre of J. G. Tajovský are held. Zvolen Castle is therefore perpetually beating with life, just like the town on which the castle watches from a small hillock.

Zvolen, nestled on the confluence of the Hron and Slatina rivers, was granted town privileges by King Belo IV in 1243. Anyway, the first written account of this area being populated comes from 1135, and includes a reference to a nearby Bleak Fort, built on an important crossroads on the trade route Via Magna.

Nowadays, we can only see ruins of the fort, hiding among trees in the forest. However, this is a paradise for archaeologists – an extensive archaeological research has been being carried out here, during which many secrets of the past have been revealed, including traces of a fortified seat dating as far back as to the late Bronze Age. Also circumstantial evidence saying that a royal fort was built here in the 12th century was confirmed.

Zvolen belongs to the oldest towns in central Slovakia, presumably because of its advantageous location. And, surely, this was the reason for crafts having flourished here in the past - especially tanners, shoemakers, tailors and potters. In the 17th century the town became famous for its cattle markets. Economic prosperity also left traces on the level of education and culture in the town. In 1940s, Zvolen was represented by

Important milestones in the town's history

1222 – the first account of Zvolen's district administrator Detricus
1232 – King Andrew II issued a document which listed royal properties in Zvolen
1243 – King Belo IV granted Zvolen with a set of town privileges
1405 – Zvolen became a free royal town
1703 – Battle of Zvolen took place
1871 – railway track was built to cross the town

Famous personalities

Valentín Balaša (1554 – 1594), poet
Jozef Kazáček (1807 – 1877), ecclesiastical dignitary
Ľudovít Štúr (1815 – 1956), writer, linguist, politician, national awakener
Mikuláš Štefan Ferenčík (1825 – 1881), writer
Ján Adolf Ferenčík (1865 – 1925), writer, editor
Jozef Cíger Hronský (1896 – 1960), writer
Mikuláš Furdík (1905 – 1967), chemist
Eugen Lehotský (1909 – 1970), painter
Eugen Pauliny (1912 – 1983), linguist
Mária Banciková (1913 – 1962), actress
Ľudo Zelienka (1917 – 1977), folk narrator
Jozef Lacko (1917 – 1978), architect
Ľudovít Fuchs (1926), poet
Milan Lasica (1940), text writer, scripter, commentator, dramatist
Ivan Kolenič (1965), poet, fiction writer

Ľudovít Štúr in Hungarian Council, which bears witness to a vigorous national life in the town. In the present, Zvolen is mainly known for being a strong centre of Slovakia's wood-working industry, with the local university and research institutions specialising in forestry, wood processing and environment.

The main square in Zvolen belongs to the largest in Slovakia. The dominant sight here is a Gothic St. Elisabeth's Church, which during restoration works in 1650 annexed Pieta Chapel on the southern side. In the chapel you can admire a lovely Baroque altar. Closer to the Zvolen Castle, in the upper part of the square, stands the Evangelical church, which was built in the neo-Gothic style in the place of former wooden little church. The whole square is fringed by several burgher houses with well-pre-

served original Renaissance and Baroque construction features. When taking a walk around here, you definitely shouldn't omit a small chateau with Rococo-decorated façade. Those who want to get more familiar with the history of forestry and wood-processing industry should visit the so-called Fink's Curia.

Even nowadays, Zvolen has a great location in terms of transport, situated near the main traffic way linking western Slovakia with the east of the country. Although being slightly sideways of the main road, Zvolen is worth stopping in – even if only for a short walk around the main town square, which breathes with both the nostalgia of the past and the energy of the present. This is what you can find only in towns peacefully nested in the bosom of splendid nature – and Zvolen definitely is one of these towns.

Places and sights worth visiting
Evangelical church
Fink's Curia
Small chateau
St. Elisabeth's Church
Town walls
Zvolen Castle

LEFT PAGE
◄ Kráľovská sieň Zvolenského zámku
► St. Elisabeth's Church

RIGHT PAGE
▲ Zvolen Castle
▼ Detail of a burgher house on the square

ŽILINA

Slovakia's Nuremberg

This is the nickname given to Žilina, the metropolis of the northwest of Slovakia, for the architectonic compactness of its oldest part - the Old Town. The integrity in terms of architecture is obvious at a first sight today, but less known is the fact that, according to archaeological findings here, the area where the city lies nowadays was populated even in the Neolithic era. The oldest found artefact giving us an account of the area of today's city is *Terra de Selinan*, dated probably 1208, a document written by Nitra province Governor Tomáš. From these times the only sight has been preserved till the present - St. Stephen's Church, located in the very centre of the Old Town. Unfortunately, no other sights and monuments have survived, as the original town was almost completely ravaged after having suffered from struggles involving feudal rulers in the late 13th century.

At the end of the 13th century, colonists from Tešín Principality (which was part of Silesia) settled in this area of the town. These newcomers began to build a new seat here in the early 14th century, and decided to take a strategically more advantageous position on the hillock over the Váh River. In those times the predecessors of the Balass family, who owned the areas around, built a fortress perhaps on the place where a parish church stood later. The centre of the fortress was a village square (nowadays Mariánske Square). These times were extraordinarily hopeful for the town and its citizens. Crafts and trade were in bloom, and Žilina became an authorised centre for many villages and smaller towns in northwest Slovakia, with the villages following Žilina laws.

But nothing in life lasts forever. When Hungarian and Polish King Lodovic I. the Great came to Žilina in May 1381, he had

1381 - the paper by King Lodovic I. the Great, Privilegium pro Slavis, issued, securing equality between Slovaks and German colonists living in the town
1451 - the first record written in Slovak language appears in the Book of Žilina

Famous personalities

Ján Milochovský, (around 1630 - 1684), Baroque writer
Hugolín Gavlovič (1712 - 1787), poet
Dušan Makovický (1866 - 1921), personal doctor of Russian writer L. N. Tolstoy
Fedor Ruppeldt (1886 - 1979), ecclesiastical dignitary, writer
Martin Hollý, Sr. (1904 - 1965), actor and director
Henrich Bartek (1907 - 1986), linguist
Ferdinand Hoffman (1908 - 1966), director and script editor

Jozef Žucha (1909 - 1964), founder of neurosurgery in Slovakia
Štefan Králik (1909 - 1983), playwright
Juraj Váh (1925 - 1976), writer
Anna Šišková (1960), film and theatre actress

Places and sights worth visiting

Budatín Castle
Burian Tower
Church of the Holy Trinity
Church of St. Paul the Apostle
Church of St. Stephen
Franciscan monastery and the Church of St. Barbara
Grand Bio Universum
Rosenfeld Palace
Žilina Synagogue

Important milestones in the town's history

1208 - the area of nowadays Žilina first mentioned in the document 'Terra de Selinan'
1312 - the first record of Žilina as a town
1321 - King Charles Robert promoted Žilina to a royal town

LEFT PAGE
◀ An extract from the Book of Žilina
▶ Budatín Castle

RIGHT PAGE
▲ The Váh River beneath Strečno Castle
◀▶ Strečno Castle
▼ Church of St. Paul the Apostle

to deal with social, economic, but mainly ethnic wrangles between Slovaks and Germans. German immigrants initially shared the power in the town with original Slovak inhabitants, but when they got richer, they were trying to push Slovaks away from the municipal authority, probably according to an old saying 'where there's money, there's power'. The King was fair, however. He had both sides heard, and made a decision that Slovaks and ethnic Germans would be represented fifty-fifty in the town council, and mayors would be elected by turns. This was how Žilina became the first town (not only in Slovakia, but also in central-eastern Europe), from where historians have an authentic document on legal equality of two ethnic groups. The document issued by King Lodovic I. the Great, Privilegium pro Slavis, thus belongs to the most precious items of

Slovak history. And when it comes to written documents, the Book of Žilina mustn't be omitted. The writing of the Book began in 1378, and it also belongs among the remarkably important documents of law, language and archives stretching even beyond the borders of Slovakia. It contains the list of the town's legal customs, based on the Magdeburg town law. Historians consider the book to be a unique written record, because it has the oldest printed entry in Slovak language in the area of Slovakia.

In the course of the centuries the town was changing mainly according to the actual situation and conditions. In 1526 the king gave the town to Burian Svetlovsky as a provisional pawn. At the turn of the 15th and 16th century Žilina ceased to be a royal town, and became a landed estate belonging to the domain of Strečno. Although Žilina only had the status of a town possessed by a squire, it kept all its free-town rights – it remained an important centre of crafts, commerce and education. Especially cloth making flourished here throughout the 16th and 17th centuries, which made the town famous in central Europe. This was also thanks to several important trade routes of international importance crossing the town, such as the well known Via Cursoris Regii (Royal Courier Route), linking Transylvania and Vienna.

The look of the town was also influenced by religious conditions. In the middle of the 16th century Žilina became the centre of Protestant movement in the Hungarian Empire. A synod was held here in 1610 during which the Evangelic Church in Slovakia was systemised for the first time ever. Tendencies towards the ideology of Reformation, together with the Renaissance spirit, were reflected in the town's architecture of those days. Bourgeois houses were being built, facing the sides of the town's main square – houses with protuberant storeys, creating arcades underneath. Also, the tree-aisle parish Church of the Holy Trinity (originally a Roman Catholic church built in Gothic style), which nowadays offers a collection of precious altar paintings. Right next to the church stands Burian Tower, was built in the first half of the 16th century, and was projected to serve as a defence tool for the town. Towards the end of the 17th century, the order of Jesuits began to act upon

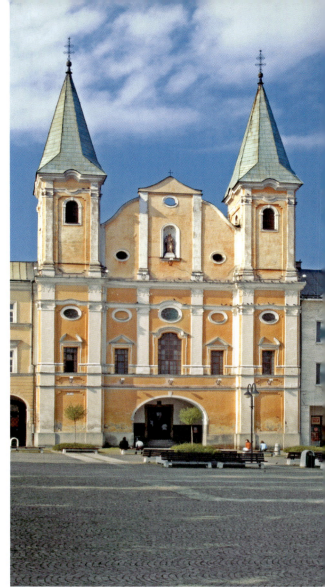

Žilina, as the order was patronised by a noble family the Esterházys. Jesuits built a two-tower church linked with a monastery on the square, and founded their own grammar school. In early 18th century Franciscans came to Žilina, and built a single-nave church without a tower (but including a monastery), in which an extremely precious Baroque decoration of interior has been preserved till the present days. To complete the list of ecclesiastical sights in the city, we shouldn't neglect the Baroque-style Marian column standing amid the square since 1738, containing a statue of the Immaculate. The column was built to pay tribute to the successfully finished process of re-Catholisation of Žilina, as well as to pay homage to one of the most dominant buildings in the city – Church of St. Paul the Apostle, built in Baroque style. As we move a few centuries forward, as far as to the early 20th century, we must also mention a synagogue built where an ancient Jewish chapel (a worship room) used to stand centuries ago. Another two impressive buildings appeared in the city during 1930s – a neo-Classicist Catholic House and the National Theatre. On the gable of the theatre building we can see a distinctive national symbol of Slovakia – containing carvings of two eagles. It was exactly this building where representatives of seven political parties signed an agreement aimed at seeing Slovakia become an autonomous state within the Czechoslovak Republic on October 6, 1938.

Not to omit any major historical points, we have to say a few more words about Budatín Castle, originally a lookout fortress coming from the 12th century and standing outside the city but belonging to it. In the past, the castle was in possession of a famous ruler Matúš Čák of Trenčín for a certain period. Later, after 1545, the next owner, Juraj Suňog, had a Renaissance water castle built around the castle's originally Romanesque-styled rounded tower. The water castle was later fine-tuned in Baroque style. The castle survived the most dramatic moments in revolutionary years of 1848 and 1849, when two battles took place here involving Slovak volunteers versus imperial soldiers and the Hungarian revolutionary army. Before Hungarians retreated on January 10, 1849, they set fire to the castle. Afterwards, the castle had to be rebuilt, and this was done in Classicist style. The contemporary look of Budatín Castle was achieved through a complete restoration in historicising style later on. The castle includes Považské Museum and a gallery offering a unique exposition of tinker craft – unique in the world.

LEFT PAGE
▲ Church of the Holy Trinity
▼ Mariánske Square

RIGHT PAGE
Burgher houses on the square

KOŠICE

The Capital of Eastern Slovakia

It's too far from Košice to Bratislava, and that's why people of eastern Slovakia consider Košice to be their capital. Actually, this is understandable, as this metropolis – with its long and rich history – had a major influence on the eastern regions of the country.

The valley along the Hornád River, lying in the Košice Basin at the foothills of the Black Mountain (Čierna Hora) and Volovské Hills, has been populated for as far back as history can trace, but the overwhelming majority of local prehistoric findings date back to the Bronze Age. As early as during Roman times, a few small settlements were established here to merge into a walled Slavic fortress later. The fortified settlement is mentioned in a document from 1230, being referred to as 'villa Cassa'. This oldest form of the city's name later changed to Latin name Cassovia, Germans called it Kaschau, Hungarians Kassa, and the Slovak form was Košice.

Like many other towns in today's Slovakia, Košice was ravaged by Tatar raids in 1241 and 1242. The recuperation came only following the arrival of colonists from Lower Saxony (today's eastern part of Germany). The settlement extended to become a walled town with good opportunities for craftsmen and merchants. The fact that the town had a significant status in terms of trade is illustrated by the existence of Košice's own coins. The oldest local coins were called marks (or, colloquially, "hrivnas"), later followed by florens, thalers and pennies. In the 14th and 15th centuries, Košice was one of five eastern Slovak towns forming an association called Pentapolitana (together with Bardejov, Prešov, Levoča and Sabinov). The town, having a number of noticeable privileges, became a spot of European importance in terms of trade and business, where wealthy merchants from all across Europe used to meet.

Important milestones in the city's history

1230 – first written record of Košice
1310 – Košice was controlled by a high royal officer Omodej; uprising
1312 – Battle of Rozhanovce
1342 – Košice was granted a set of privileges, ranking it among the most important towns in the kingdom
1556 – another, even more devastating fire destroyed the town almost completely
1657 – Jesuit University was established
1804 – Košice diocese was established
1860 – the first railroad was built in Košice
1918 – the town became part of the Czechoslovak Republic
1938 – Košice was annexed to Horthy's Hungary
1945 – so-called Košice Government Manifesto was declared here
1960 – construction of Košice's steelworks was launched

Famous personalities

Imrich Henszelmann (1813 – 1888), archeologist, art historian
Vojtech Gerster (1850 – 1923), architect of the Corinth Canal and co-architect of the Panama Canal
Ján Kňazovický (1893 – 1987), doctor
Sándor Márai (1900 – 1989), writer
Július Jakoby (1903 – 1985), painter
Vojtech Löffler (1906 - 1990), sculptor
Alina Ferdinandyová (1926 – 1974), sculptress
Jozef Psotka (1934 – 1984), mountaineer
Andrej Kvašňák (1936), football player
Jozef Gönci (1974), world champion in marksmanship
Martina Hingis (1980), tennis player

Places and sights worth visiting
Andrássy Palace
Bishop's Residence
Csáky Palace
Dome of St. Elisabeth (St. Elisabeth's Cathedral)
East Slovak Museum
Forgáč Palace
Former House of the Chamber – Gallery of Julius
   Jakoby
Former Synagogue – ''The House of Arts''
Former Town Hall
Jakab Palace
Levoča House

Rákóczi Palace – Slovak Technical Museum
The State Theatre
Urban's Tower

LEFT PAGE

▲ One the precious Gothic panel paintings from 1526
   (East Slovak Museum)

◄ Košice's gold treasure

► Detail of the altar in St. Elisabeth's Cathedral

RIGHT PAGE

St. Elisabeth's Cathedral

The people of Košice always fought for their rights, when necessary, in order to maintain the town's favourable status. In 1304, they were pitted against Omodej Abo, a high royal officer who had control of extensive lands of today's eastern Slovakia. Abo and his western ally Matúš Čák of Trenčín were the leading objectors towards the Royal Crown, which was then in the hands of King Charles Robert. Košice was the king's ally in the memorable Battle of Rozhanovce in 1312. Following victory, the ruler rewarded Košice with granting it town privileges. In 1342, Košice was granted another important privilege - that of becoming a free royal town. And when talking about historical landmarks - on May 7, 1369, Košice became the first European town to be granted an armorial decree signed by king. This day is celebrated in the town even in the present - as the Day of Košice.

The town was gradually getting richer and stronger due to its crafts and commerce, so it had enough money to spend on building sumptuous cathedrals and minsters. These were Gothic times, and this artistic style influenced the buildings erected in Košice the most. Soon, the famous local Gothic highlight - St. Elisabeth's Cathedral (also called the Dome of St. Elisabeth) - was sticking out from behind the town walls. This monumental architectonic work, on which the works took more than a century, was, in its in-

itial construction phases, supported by King Charles Robert himself, who enjoyed being in the good graces of the Pope. One of Charles Robert's wives was Polish-born Elisabeth Piast. She was extraordinarily interested in how the works on the dome were progressing. Historical documents even say that she took the town under her aegis, and often visited it on her journeys to her home country, Poland. The cathedral was named after a younger sister of a former king Belo IV, St. Elisabeth, who was a predecessor of Elisabeth Piast's family. This was one of the reasons why she was so fond of the dome. Nowadays, the Dome of St. Elisabeth has two interesing primacies - it's the biggest and at the same time the most easterly church/cathedral of the western type in Europe. Especially the main altar here deserves our attention, as it contains the biggest set of Gothic panel paintings in Europe.

This peaceful period in the town's history ended in the first half of the 15th century, with a number of events related to a series of struggles for the Hungarian throne. Following 1440, Košice became the seat of Czech-born

LEFT PAGE
Interior of St. Elisabeth's Cathedral

RIGHT PAGE
▲ Urban's Tower, dated 14th century
▼ Historical street car in the city centre

Ján Jiskra of Brandýs, and thus witnessed his military raids all around Hungary and Poland. Moreover, most of the town was devastated by an extensive fire in 1556.

Following the fire, architectonic dominance in Košice dramatically shifted – Gothic changed to Renaissance. In the years to come Košice was largely influenced by the Reformation Movement, and the town was turned into an almost unassailable fortress. Following this period, it happened to directly witness a number of riots, revolts and uprisings stemming from the tension between the Hungarian Estates and military forces backing the interests of the ruling Hapsburgs. The only positive asset in those years was the establishment of the Jesuit University – then the most easterly European university – which turned into the Royal Academy in 1776.

Much more peaceful period for Košice was the 18th century, carrying the spirit of intensive recatholisation. A century later, in the early 19th century, the spiritual position of the town was even strengthened following

the establishment of the local diocese (bishopric). However, the town copied the overall social and political development in the Austrian-Hungarian Empire – it became the centre of Hungarian Uprising held against Vienna, and during the period of the industrial revolution manufacturing operations were sprouting up here: mainly producers of English porcelain, hats and drapery. Also, many sumptuous houses of well-to-do townsmen were built here during this period. Košice couldn't avert the necessary political changes at the beginning of the 20th century. On the last day in 1918, the city was included in the Czechoslovak Republic, and in 1938 was swallowed by (Admiral Horthy's) Hungary for the next six years. After liberation in April 1945, the Czechoslovak government met in Košice to issue the so-called Košice Government Manifesto, dealing with the post-war setup of the republic. Following this, Košice became a modern city – also thanks to the biggest factory established in Slovakia, Východoslovenské železiarne (East Slovak Ironworks).

LEFT PAGE
▲ Aristocratic palaces and burgher houses on the square
▼ University Church from the 17th century

RIGHT PAGE
Janko Borodáč Theatre

BARDEJOV

The Town So Rich and Rigid

In medieval times the town of Bardejov was known for the severity of its justice system, and the local Book of Judgements, kept in the municipal archives today, bears witness to this fact. The book mentions someone at the stake for stealing honey and destroying a beehive, cutting someone's head off for another theft, and even crucifixion for robbing the mayor's house. Apart from this, the house in which local executioners used to live had a special position among the houses at the end of Väzničná (Prison) Street. In the Basilica of St. Egidius, a pew where executioners used to sit (separated from the others) can be seen even today. And if you want to see where the executioners used to carry out the decapitations, check out the Lamp Column, so-called 'Kopfstock'. Nowadays, we only assume that it was in part thanks to these strict justice measures that Barde-

jov thrived, and ranked among the richest Slovak towns for many centuries.

The actual inception of the ancient town is a bit sketchy, of course. But, according to historians, it dates back as far as the 11th century, with the first written record of its existence coming only from 13th century, when a certain settlement called Bardauev is mentioned in the Ipatijev Chronicle. Another historical document, dated six years after the record from the chronicle, reads that there is a Cistercian monastery in the area of '*Terra Bardpha*'. At any rate, by the end of the 14th century Bardejov had grown up thanks to its advantageous location, being a stop-off point on a trading route. The town was fortunate to have been granted a number of royal privileges in that period, no doubt thanks to its skilful craftsmen and clever merchants, whose business determination turned Bardejov in-

LEFT PAGE
▲ Building of the former Town Hall from the 16th century stands in the square.
◀ Side altar in the Church of St. Egidius
▶ Gothic Church of St. Egidius – a national cultural monument

RIGHT PAGE
Interior of the Church of St. Egidius

Important milestones in the town's history
1241 – settlement referred to as 'Bardouev' was mentioned in the Ipatijev Chronicle
1376 – Bardejov was promoted to a free royal town
1878 – Bardejov hit by an extensive fire
2000 – the town was included in UNESCO's World Heritage List

Famous personalities
Leonard Stöckel (1510 – 1560), teacher, author of religious writing
Jakub Zabler (1639 – 1709), clerical dignitary
Ľudovít Absolon (1909 – 1988), photographer
Professors at Bardejov's lyceum – J. Chalupka, K. Kuzmány
Students at the lyceum – M. Šulek, G. Fejérpataky-Belopotocký, P. J. Šafárik, S. Chalupka, D. Lichard, C. Zoch, A. H. Škultéty, J. Kráľ, J. Záborský, P. Bohúň, P. Országh-Hviezdoslav, L. Nádaši-Jégé, M. Kukučín, P. Dobšinský, J. Jesenský, M. Rázus, I. Stodola and others

Places and sights worth visiting
Bardejov Spa
Bardejov's town walls
Church of St. Egidius
Evangelical church
Executioner's House
Fountain with the Statue of St. Florian
Gantzughof House (today the seat of Šariš Museum)
Greco-Catholic Church of St. Peter and Paul
Jewish synagogue
Monastery and the Church of St. John the Baptist
Museum of Šariš Folk Architecture
Radničné Square (in front of the Town Hall)

which became famous world-wide for the therapeutic effects of its acidic local waters.

The first bloom of the spa was seen in early 19th century, when Hungarian and Polish aristocracy frequently visited this health resort. Austrian Princess Maria Louise (wife-to-be of Napoleon Bonaparte) was here in 1809, Russian Tsar Alexander I spent a few weeks here in 1821, and popular Austrian Empress Elisabeth visited the spa in the summer of 1895.

In the beginning of the 20th century, the Bardejov Spa was among the best known spas with the best facilities in the whole Austro-Hungarian empire.

to one of the most prominent royal towns in the Hungarian Empire. The highlight of all privileges granted to the town came in 1376, when King Ludovicus I decided to promote Bardejov to a free royal city. Also throughout the 15th century the town enjoyed being supported by Hungarian kings, notably Sigmund Luxembourg and Matthias Corvinus.

This century represents the golden age of Bardejov. The town was at the peak of its economic development, with a remarkable construction boom throughout the 15th century. First of all, the rich town finished construction of its parish church, and furnished it with some new altars. Then, people began to build a representative building – the Town Hall – in the central part of the town's square.

If the 15th century was the blaze of glory for the town, it is the 16th century in which culture and education flourished. To a large extent this was thanks to the arrival of the Reformation movement, the ideas of which were compliantly absorbed by the mainly German patricians of the town. Especially Bardejov-born Leonard Stöckel, a student of Martin Luther and a friend of Filip Melanchton, was disseminating the ideas born in Germany. Stöckel founded a Latin school in Bardejov, where he personally tutored youths who came from all around the country – in keeping with the spirit of humanism and enlightenment. The school

had a very good reputation, and among its students were, for example, famous Slovak humanist poet Martin Rakovský and author of religious writing Štefan Pilárik. The school building (1538) stands right next to the church.

The 17th century meant a less sanguine period for Bardejov, as it became over-shadowed by the more successful town Prešov. But the succeeding centuries were more ambitious for Bardejov. Jewish merchants helped Bardejov a great deal by building a synagogue, followed by a ritual spa building, a school and a congregation hall.

A devastating fire in 1878 made the next reconstruction of the town a forced one, unfortunately. Later, the town finished construction of the railway station (1890), and the railway track connected Bardejov with Prešov and other towns in the Hungarian Empire.

In 1950, Bardejov was officially declared a municipal site for preservation, and much has been done to keep it in authentic and good condition since then. Being the first town in the former Czechoslovakia, Bardejov in 1986 received an award for conservation activities from the International Curatorship – a Gold Medal for the revival of its site. In addition, it was included in UNESCO's World Heritage List in 2000.

Any picture of Bardejov would not be complete without mentioning the local spa,

HUMENNÉ

Marian Cult, Hope and Faith

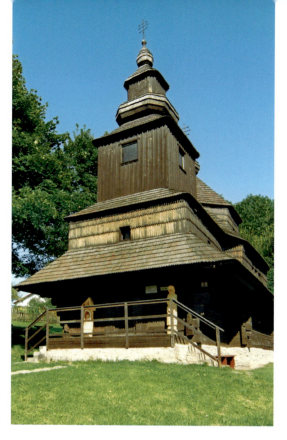

An unusual local man greets visitors to the town of Humenné arriving by train as, under a tree near the platform, stands a statue of Švejk. Any reference to the work is impossible without innumerable cross-reference as those who have carefully read the unforgettable novel 'Good Soldier Švejk' by Jaroslav Hašek will know. Particularly careful readers will recall the dialogue that takes place at the train station in Humené, where he finds the "excellent ferriferous waters". Thus Švejk made Humenné a known town.

Humenné is also original in its location, in the middle of Europe, lying between Slovakia's towns Košice and Prešov, Poland's Jaslo, Sub-Carpathian towns Mukachevo and Uzhghorod in Ukraine, Hungary's Nyiregyháza, and Romania's Satu Mare. The fate of the town and its surroundings has been determined by the Laborec River and Carpathian Hills, and has always been under the volcanic Vihorlat Mountains. Due to advantageous location and mild climate, the surroundings of where Humenné is now were populated ever since the Stone Age, to

which local archaeological findings bear witness. Slavs began coming to the basin of Humenné in the 5th century, during the period known as the Great Migration. The first written record of the town dates back to 1317. The history of Humenné is closely connected with a prominent noble Italian family, the Drugeths, who came to the Hungarian Empire in the early 14th century, accompanied by King Charles Robert of Anjou. These distinguished aristocrats turned Humenné into one of the biggest feudal domains in whole of Slovakia, while in the 15th century King Matthias Corvinus granted the town with privileges affirmed by the seal and coat of arms. In those times, the town was an important stop-off point on the trade route linking Hungary and Poland.

In almost every town and city, architectonic sights complement the history and Humenné is no exception in this respect. In the place of former stone fort in Humenné, a Rernaissance castle was erected around 1610, and today remains one of the most significant sights in the town. It

LEFT PAGE
▲ Wooden church in Nová Sedlica
◄ Interior of a rustic house
► Open-air Museum of Folk Architecture

RIGHT PAGE
▲ Renaissance chateau from 1610
▼ Interior of the chateau

Important milestones in the town's history
1313 – Jesuit Collegium was established
1317 – the first written record of the town

1610 – Renaissance castle was built in the place of former stone fort
1684 – the Drugeths died off
1871 – completion of the local railroad

Famous personalities
Ladislav Grosman (1921 – 1977), writer
Dušan Kováč (1942), historian, writer
Milan Lechan (1943), humorist, poet
Jozef Žarnay (1944), children's fiction writer
Mikuláš Kočan (1946), playwright, poet
Václav Pankovčín (1968 – 1999), writer

Places and sights worth visiting
Franciscan monastery and church
Gothic Roman-Catholic Franciscan church
Humenné's Castle – the Vihorlat Museum
Observatory
Open-air Museum of Folk Architecture
Wooden Church of St. Michael Archangel

gained its contemporary look in the late 19th century, when owned by the Andrássys, a wealthy aristocratic family. At the restoration works then, it was given shape and structure according to French Baroque castles, plus an English park (including a fishpond) was built near it. The castle's gate has been decorated by the sculptures of lion and lioness. In its interior (rooms where the Vihorlat Museum is seated today) you can admire period furniture and a painting that features former owners of the castle.

Humenné has always lived spiritually, and the first written record of the town's religious life comes from 1332. By this year, the town must have already had a brick parish church built, which was sacrificed to St. Peter, and which was burned out in 1778. In the 14th century, Franciscan monks built a monastery and a church on the outskirts of the town and dedicated it to Virgin Mary, and this represents the beginnings of the Marian cult in Humenné.

The story behind the altar painting of Our Lady of Seven Sorrows is interesting. When the Franciscan monks were forced to leave the town (due to upcoming Reformation movement), they wanted to save the painting and so it was taken to a monastery in Po-

land. Although the Franciscans returned to their monastery in 1656, they didn't dedicate the church to the Virgin Mary. Instead, with financial assistance from local esquires, the monks built a chapel near the church, and this chapel was dedicated to Virgin Mary Loretan, the Queen of Angels. But the painting didn't come back from Poland. Eventually, the people of Humenné built a side altar where they put another painting featuring the Virgin Mary. The chapel became a well-known site, a destination of pilgrimages. People coming here sometimes used to bring various body parts made of wax, which symbolized parts of their bodies that they had health problems with. These wax objects were put in front of the painting, in hopes of a healthy recovery.

In the castle's garden you can find an open-air Museum of Folk Architecture, where you can get familiar with architectonic traditions and skills of people from this region. But the real highlight attracting your attention will be the wooden Church of St. Michael Archangel, which was brought here from the village of Nová Sedlica. Apart from the fact that it's completely wooden, it's famous for having originally been built without a single nail.

KEŽMAROK

Pearl under the High Tatras

Perhaps no other Slovak town has had so many names as Kežmarok in the past. Often, the people of Kežmarok themselves didn't know which of more than 150 names to use. The incredible list includes, for example, names such as Kaszmark, Kysmark, Kesmarek and Tyropolis. People often debated the merits of these names, but there's no clue to find out which bears the most authenticity.

This cultural and historical town lying just beneath the foothills of the High Tatras is widely known for its sights as well as its hospitality. And there's one more typical feature that Kežmarok has – three ethnic groups used to live here peacefully for centuries: Slovaks, Germans and Hungarians. Who had lived here even before them is best illustrated by archaeological findings.

On the so-called Jerusalem Hill, lying on the outskirts of the town, artefacts coming from the Stone Age, the Bronze Age and the Iron Age, as well as Roman and Celtic coins were found, all representing probably the oldest objects relevant to the population of this area. According to some sources, the town was allegedly mentioned in 1190, when Levoča-based chronicler Gašpar Hain could have made a reference to a convent standing in the place where the local castle stands today. However, solid and reliable evidence of the first written record of Kežmarok is represented by the document issued by King Belo IV in 1251. The town was formed from four settlements, where people of different ethnicity lived. The first one was a Slovak settlement near the Church of St. Michael, also inhabited by Hungarians as protectors of the border with Poland. The second settlement was populated by Germans and located near the Church of St. Elisabeth. The third settlement was another Slovak one, spreading

Important milestones in the town's history
1251 – the first record of Kežmarok
1269 – Kežmarok was granted town privileges
1380 – Kežmarok became a free royal town

Famous personalities
Ján and Krištof Lang (1st half of the 16th century), artistic carvers
Dávid Fröhlich (1595 – 1648), geographer and astronomer
Imrich Thököly (1657 – 1705), leader of an anti-Hapsburg uprising
Juraj Buchholtz (1668 – 1737), natural scientist
Daniel Fischer (1695 – 1746), natural scientist
Ján Daniel Perlitzi (1705 – 1778), doctor, natural scientist
Fridrich Hažlinský (1818 – 1896), botanist
Vojtech Alexander (1857 – 1916), pioneer of röntgenology (X-ray studies) and radiology in Hungarian Empire
Anton Pridavok (1904 – 1945), poet and fiction writer

Places and sights worth visiting
Church of Our Lady
Church of the Saint Cross
Evangelical wooden church
Kežmarok Castle
Museum
New Evangelical church
Townsmen's House

around the Church of the Saint Cross, while the fourth was simply referred to as 'the settlement of Peter and Paul' (presumably referring to its location near the Church of St. Peter and Paul). Owing to security reasons, all four settlements merged into one town, which was already walled in 1368.

Kežmarok became a free royal town in the 15th century. At that time it was granted quite a number of economic and political privileges, such as the right of sword, to use its own coat of arms, to hold two annual markets, as well as the right to have its own stocks. Just because of the latter right, Kežmarok was warring Levoča for a century, as having own stocks was of great importance to Kežmarok, given that the town was crossed by an important trade route leading from the Orient to the north of Europe. Local guilds also contributed to the pace of the town's development. Between the 15th and the 19th centuries, there were around forty craft guilds, the best known were cloth makers, weavers, dyers, carpenters and goldsmiths.

On the other hand, economically thriving Kežmarok suffered plague epidemics and had to survive frequent fires. The Church of St. Michael was brought down in 1433, and when the Hussites left Kežmarok, the locals rebuilt the town walls firstly, and in 1461 began to rebuild the parish Church of the Saint Cross, plus they laid the foundation stone of the future town hall building. The town recuperated when Kežmarok Castle was completed in 1463, which was built as part of the town walls. The castle represented not only an impressive and dominant sight in terms of urbanism and architecture, but also brought positive socio-economic effects. However, soon after it was completed, it became the subject of various disputes and tensions, because its owners wanted to take control of the whole town. The best illustration of this is when the Thökölys, a noble Hungarian family, arrived in Kežmarok. The result was truculence, daily robberies and street fights.

Starting in mid-17th century, the town was trying to get out from under the rule of the local squire, in which it succeeded when the Vienna Pact was signed. In 1655, Kežmarok was promoted to a free royal town, and after the fall of the Thökölys in 1687 the town took control of the castle and their lands. Kežmarok Castle nowadays belongs to the best-preserved castles in the Spiš area.

Apart from the castle, Kežmarok is proud of several other sights, including a late-Gothic Church of the Saint Cross, which was built between 1444 and 1498 and sponsored by the Zápoľský family. It stands in the place where an old chapel had stood before. The church includes the main altar (made of wood) with carvings by Master Paul of Levoča. In front of the church you can admire a lone-standing bell tower from 1568, which is considered to be the oldest Renaissance bell tower in Slovakia.

Kežmarok has two national cultural monuments. The first one is Evangelical Lyceum, which has one of the largest school libraries in central Europe. The library has some 150,000 books, of which around 3,000 date as far back as the 16th century. The other national cultural monument is an Evangelical wooden church from 1717, built based on the model of an Amsterdam timber church. The church's uniqueness lies in the fact that not a single piece of metal was used during its construction, the interior is completely made of yew and red spruce. Also, an organ with wooden pipes is worth seeing here.

LEVOČA

The Lambent Jewel on the Spiš Crown

The old town Levoča, already in medieval times, was of European importance and today it can well be included in the list of world's treasures. The town was made famous, and still is, especially thanks to its native Master Paul of Levoča, who is rightfully considered to be Slovakia's greatest and the most brilliant medieval artist. According to historical documents available, Master Paul worked here as of 1506, run-ning a big local workshop where a number of remarkable cravers, painters and gold-smiths worked. Following some other hy-potheses, he previously had been working in the shop run by Master Ansus in Sab-inov, and was also active in Banská Bystri-ca. Historians assume that he might have been invited to Levoča by local townsmen, who in 1515 elected him one of the leaders of the Fraternity of the Divine Body. Dur-

Important milestones in the town's history

1249 – the first record of the town (referred to as 'Leucha')
1271 – Levoča was promoted to become the capital of the Fellowship of Saxons in Spiš
1323 – Levoča was declared a free royal town

Famous personalities:
Master Paul of Levoča (around 1470 – around 1540), famous craver
Dávid Fröhlich (1595 – 1648), geographer, astronomer
Daniel Sinapius-Horčička (1640 – 1688), writer
Ján Szilassy (1705 – 1782), goldsmith
Maximilán Hell (1720 – 1792), physicist and astronomer
Jozef Sklenár (1746 – 1790), historian
Jozef Caucik (1780 – 1875), painter
Ján Rombauer (1782 – 1849), painter
Gašpar Fajérpataky-Belopotocký (1794 – 1874), publisher and co-founder of the first amateur theatre group in Slovakia
Janko Matuška (1821 – 1877), poet
Ján Francisci-Rimavský (1822 – 1905), writer and translator

Mikuláš Dohnány (1824 – 1852), playwright and historian
Pavol Dobšinský (1828 – 1885), folklorist, writer, poet and translator
Ján Botto (1829 – 1881), poet

Places and sights worth visiting
Church of Holy Spirit
Church of St. James
Master Paul's House
Master Paul's Square
Minorite Monastery
Spiš Museum
St. George's Chapel
Thurzo's House (16th century)

ing the period spanning almost forty years that he spent in the Spiš area, he created carvings belonging to the best works of late Gothic in Europe.

The works of Master Paul of Levoča are unique and remarkable not only in terms of their artistic merit and extent, but also because of their massive influence on his followers.

What provided Master Paul the opportunity to fully develop his craving skills? The answer can be found in the history of Levoča, which goes back as far as the 13th century. The first written record comes from 1249, when the town is mentioned under the name Leucha. Archaeological findings prove that the area where Levoča lies today has been populated since that time.

Soon after the first record in the documents, Levoča gained several privileges, including the right to hold markets and collect tolls. At that time colonists probably populated the town, and only later did it become an important centre lying on the trade route leading from Hungary to Poland, aided by a profitable business environment, as well as rulers who granted the town further political and economic privileges. This period represented the financial bloom of Levoča, and its social life was flourishing in all respects. This was apparent manly in the rapid development of architecture, education, culture, and arts and crafts. In 1550 and 1599 the town survived extensive fires; nonetheless, it managed to keep its respectable position until the end of the 16th century. Levoča was in those times the centre of Reformation Movement in Slovakia, and as of 1624 Breuer's printing office was running here, and engaged in editorial activities. Comenius's masterpiece 'Orbis Pictus' was printed here in four languages in 1685.

Levoča has kept this historical-cultural dimension, and the town and its sights is among the most beautiful in Slovakia. The town's central square includes more than fifty Gothic, Renaissance and early-Baroque houses with arcades built in their interior yards. The historical core of the town is fringed by parts of the former town walls from the 14th and the 15th centuries that are some two kilometres long. Church of St. James, which is the second biggest church in Slovakia, is of a unique character. In total, we find here eleven Gothic and Renaissance altars, of which the main altar is the most valuable, made between 1508 and 1517. With its height of 18.6 metres and width of 6 metres, it's the highest late-Gothic wooden altar in the world. Of course, it was none other than Master Paul who made it. This unique work of art is a national cultural monument. Another two altars in the church were brought by Master Paul, as was the equestrian statue of St. George located in the northern chapel of the church.

Next to the church stands the building of former town hall, a symbol of town privileges and independence of Levoča, which belongs among the best secular Renaissance architectural works in Slovakia. In front of the building, there's the so-called 'Cage of Shame' dating back to the turn of the 16th and 17th century, which was used for public punishment of miscreants and misbehaving wives. This place usually turns into a theatre stage during the summer, giving us a chance to view the sad tale of the White Lady of Levoča (set in the early 18th century, when the town was beleaguered by the Imperial army). Legend has it that

the sad ghost of Julia was last seen roaming in Levoča – dressed in white (hence 'the White Lady').

Of many sacral sights that we can admire in the town, we shouldn't miss the Old Minorite Monastery (of which only a few original rooms have survived, including the Gothic Cloister), and the so-called New Minorite Monastery with its untouched interior featuring valuable frescos. Levoča is the biggest pilgrimage destination in Slovakia, annually visited by believers from all around the world journeying to worship Virgin Mary.

LEFT PAGE
▲ Church of St. James
▼ Detail of the main altar, carved by Master Paul of Levoča

RIGHT PAGE
◄ Thurzo's House
► Part of the main altar in the Church of St. James, by Master Paul of Levoča

MICHALOVCE

Bird Paradise on Earth

The Lower Zemplín area, the centre of which is the town of Michalovce, mainly became known thanks to its large local dam called Zemplínska šírava. Visitors to the region usually first go to there to relax in its natural environment, and only then go sightseeing in Michalovce. Let's begin our trip with a walk outside the town, then. Michalovce lies in the northern part of the East Slovak Lowland, and is from both sides being overseen by forested mounds Hrádok and Biela hora.

East Slovak Lowland has always enjoyed more than its fair share of sunshine, with meteorologists counting up to 240 sunny days a year here. Rare, interesting and lovely to the eye is the area around the village of Senné (in Michalovce district) - the local swamplands, fens and trenches have long been a junction of the migratory-bird routes. Every year more than 150 bird species stop

here to rest, and then fly on. As one third of them also nests here, the site has been put on the international list of significant localities in terms of bird protection. The eastern side of Zemplínska Šírava Dam is also considered to be ornithologist's paradise. It's a protected- bird reserve, because nearly 100 waterfowl species live here, with many of them being rare and protected.

Detailed information concerning nature, but also society and arts in this region, are available in Zemplín Museum in Michalovce. The building in which the museum is installed is highly symbolic: it's a rotunda from the times of Great Moravian Empire – a great place for a museum, indeed. In the museum we can find some remarkable natural exposits. Plus the archaeological exposition installed here is of great value, including the array of golden pendants (the oldest evidence concerning the treatment

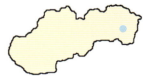

Important milestones in the town's history
1244 – the first written record on the name of the town
1418 – Michalovce became the centre of four
    districts belonging under Zemplín region

1828 – forty-nine craftsmen's workshops
1867 – Michalovce became administrative seat
    of the district
1871 – railroad was built

Famous personalities
Gorazd Zvonický (1913 – 1995), write
Pavol Horov (1914 - 1975), poet r
Jozef Puškáš (1951), writer
Miroslav Halás (1954), writer
Martin Vladík (1960), poet
Maroš Bančej (1961), poet

Places and sights worth visiting
Greco-Catholic Church of Holy Spirit
Greco-Catholic Church of Our Lady
Roman-Catholic Church of Virgin Mary
Viniansky Castle
Zemplínska Šírava Dam
Zemplín Museum

▲ Surroundings of Michalovce are
important bird sanctuaries.
◄ Greco-Catholic church
► Valuable archaeological
finding – a Celtic jar

of gold in Slovakia) and an amphora (from Bronze Age) with the oldest feature of two-wheeled carriage in central Europe. Another exposition in the museum is ethnographical, which offers documented history of pottery in a nearby village of Pozdišovce. The village is known for using the typical Zemplín folk costumes, but became famous in Slovakia and even abroad for its production of lovely ceramic objects. Pottery has a long tradition here – the first report on the locals being engaged in pottery and tile-making is evidenced as far back as 1416, and the history of pottery guild began here in 1743. It's interesting that local potters used to build their kilns either as caves dug in hills, or as cone-shaped kilns located in backyards, so that they could be used by several craft masters. Later, potters' focus shifted from applied-art objects towards unique art-ceramics products.

The best historical-cultural highlight worth seeing in Michalovce is a manor house standing on the embankment lining the Laborec River. Originally, a water castle from the 13th century used to stand here, built to repel potential enemies and threats. The castle included a Gothic block with corner towers, but this look was changed during a restoration works in the Renaissance spirit. The most apparent architectonic feature nowadays is an arcade with a balcony on the frontage of the house. From among the sacral sights in Michalovce, the original Gothic Roman-Catholic Church of Virgin Mary as well as Greco-Catholic churches (Church of Our Lady and Church of Holy Spirit) are also worth checking out.

An interesting thing about the town is the story of its name. The record from 1244 has it as 'Myhal' (apparently related to the name 'Michael'), while as of 1284 the town used to be referred as Nogmihal (meaning something like 'big Michael'). It was only as of 1773 that the town was named as we call it now, but in Polish form – Michalowcze.

Anyway, more problematic than the town's name were the transportation routes to and from Michalovce in the past, but things rapidly improved after building the railroad in 1871. The town improved economically, entrenching commerce and agriculture, as well as establishing the groundwork for the development of the food industry. After the end of WWII, the town continued in a relatively fine pace of prosperity, introducing textile, engineering and clay ware industries.

In the sphere of culture, Michalovce is proud of its professional folk group Zemplín and of holding an annual folk event Zemplín Festival of Songs and Dances.

▲ Historical chateau is the seat of Zemplín Museum.
▼ Zemplínska Šírava Dam

PODOLÍNEC

Junction of Gothic and Renaissance

Walking down the alleys of Podolínec is like leafing through a book of archives, with every single page being a precious artefact documenting periods of history – but, most of all, providing documented evidence of people's lives. It's people who create history, creating a unique mosaic through their activities. It's a mosaic that later becomes a subject of admiration by their descendants, who further refine it. This has been, and still is, the case of the mosaic of Podolínec, a little town nested in the valley of the Poprad River, on the edge of Spišská Magura highland area, the Sub-Tatras Basin and the Levoča Hills.

The town's history was somewhat predetermined by its location, as the area it spreads out over has, since ancient times, been a buffer zone where Polish and Hungarian sovereignties met. So the past of the town is linked to both countries' histories. The original Slavic settlement of Podolínec was ravaged by Tatars in 1241 and 1244, and was re-founded no sooner than in the second half of the 13th century. More than a century later, in 1412, King Sigmund Luxemburg promoted it to become a free royal town, which meant that it gained the same status as the towns Levoča and Kežmarok, and this gesture of goodwill allowed the town to hold weekly markets and annual fairs. Crafts and trade were flourishing in the town in those days, and the most famous was the production of knives with preciously decorated handgrips. However, the very same year Podolínec, together with another 16 towns of the Spiš region, was pawned off and found itself in the hands of Polish King Vladislav II for as long as 300 years. Afraid of the Hussites, King Sigmund in 1422 located military units all around the region, with one of them placed in Podolínec. Thanks to this, Podolínec, unlike other towns (which were stagnating), was doing well.

The town's historical core has retained its original structure till today. The structure is closely related to the town's Gothic-Renaissance historical roots. The oldest building

1990 – Podolínec was declared a municipal sight reservation

Famous personalities
Sigismundus Senftleben from Podolínec (died before 1514), author of a dictionary for preachers
Valér Berzevici (1646 – 1707), playwright, pedagogue, since 1670 a member of Piarist order in Podolínec

Places and sights worth visiting
Church of Assumption
Piarist monastery and church
St. Ann's Chapel

LEFT PAGE
▲ Bell-tower with precious bell from 1392
▼ Renaissance burgher houses on the square

RIGHT PAGE
▲▼ Piarist monastery

in Podolinec is St. Ann's Chapel, a Gothic church dating back to the turn of the 13th and the 14th centuries that stands at the local cemetery, which lies northwest of the town today. In view of this relative distance, one can assume how extensive the area of the then settlement must have been. Also, it's supposed that the town's fortification, built from 1295, ringed the thickly-populated parts of the settlement, and the town itself used to spread out over the area where it lies now to a large extent. In 1295, a new Church of Assumption was built around the marketplace. The church later underwent a number of architectonic emendations. In the chancel of the church, we can see precious Gothic wall paintings ap-

plied in several layers, all from between 1380 – 1430. Valuable is also a sculpted main altar (from 1700 – 1710) and a Gothic baptismal font (from the latter half of the 14th century). In 1659, a Renaissance bell tower was built next to the church, with a precious bell which dates back to 1392. Later, in the mid-17th century, an early-Baroque Piarist monastery with a double-towered church were added to the existing scenery .

These monuments still create the winsome skyline of the town. The local well-preserved urbanistic-architectonic sights and the town's romantic alleys are unique in all Slovakia, so it's no wonder that Podolinec was declared a municipal sight reservation in 1990.

POPRAD AND THE TATRAS

The Angel Captured by Beauty

Do you know why Slovakia's loveliest peak – Kriváň – tilts on one side? A legend has it that when the God created the world, he sent an angel to check out if there's no place on Earth he had forgotten about. When flying over the Tatras, captured by the beauty, the angel hit against a peak that was later given name Kriváň. The name is derived from Slovak word for 'bent, uneven, crooked' – 'krivý'. The area of the Tatra Mountains is the landscape full of high rocky peaks, deep valleys, splendid tarns – simply a unique land with its breathtaking magnificence and singularities of its natural scenery. If we wanted to count all the hills and peaks out there, it would be a long list. The best known Slovak fairy-tale writer Pavol Dobšinský wrote that there are 999 hillsides in the Tatras, which was an estimate not far from the real number.

The highest, jaggiest and loveliest of the whole Tatra massif are the High Tatras, where the highest hill in Slovakia spreads. It's the Gerlach Peak, 2,654-metres high in altitude. Another nine hills with their heights exceeding 2,600 metres in altitude surround it. Accessible to the public is the third highest of them – the Lomnický Peak rising to 2,634 metres above the sea level, where we can get by taking cableway. Due to their almost always coldest, wettest and windiest weather in Slovakia, on the old maps the Tatras used to be referred to as 'Schneeberg', a German word meaning 'snowy hills'. In fact, snow cover is kept here much longer than elsewhere in the country throughout a year. In some valleys you can see snow even in the middle of summer.

Pioneer of discovering the natural treasures of the Tatras was a Slovak natural scientist, teacher and preacher Juraj Buchholtz, Sr. who in 1664 climbed up the Slavkovský Peak. In his later works, he depicted in details the natural scenery, mineral resources and flora in the

Important milestones in the town's history
1256 – the first written record of Poprad
1412 – the town was pawned to Poland

Famous personalities
Juraj Buchholtz, Sr. (1643 – 1724), natural scientist, teacher
Samuel Augustini (1729 – 1792), explorer
Gregor Berzevica (1763 – 1822), economist
Viliam Aurel Scherfel (1835 – 1895), founder of the Sub-Tatras Museum
Vladimír Roy (1885 – 1936), poet
Gustáv Nedobrý (1893 – 1966), one of the founders of the mountaineering club
Ján Jamnický (1908 – 1972), actor, film director, teacher
Maša Haľamová (1908 – 1995), poet

Places and sights worth visiting
Around Poprad and in the High Tatras:
Church of St. Stephen the King in the village of Matejovce
Podbanské and surroundings
Smokovce and surroundings
Štrbské Pleso (Štrbské Tarn) and surroundings
Tatranská Javorina and surroundings
Tatranská Kotlina and surroundings
Tatranská Lomnica and surroundings
Vyšné Hágy, Nová Polianka and Tatranská Polianka
Ždiar and surroundings
In Poprad:
Church of St. Egidius
Church of St. John the Evangelist
Sub-Tatras Museum

LEFT PAGE
◄ The square: Evangelic church
► Ďumbier

RIGHT PAGE
▲ High Tatras
▼ Renaissance bell-tower on the square, dated 1658

Tatras. Interesting enough is the fact that, the first tourist to the Tatras – even before Buchholtz – was a woman. It was Princess Beáta Laská from the castle in Kežmarok. In 1565, she and several people from Kežmarok set off on a trip towards the Snowy Hills. When the princess returned home, she had to atone for her courage – her angry husband locked her in the castle tower for the next six years. From the tower, through a small window, she had only a limited view of her beloved Tatras. Anyway, that was the 16th century. In the present, the Tatras are a sought-after tourist paradise for the visitors to Slovakia.

The High Tatras are sometimes called 'the smallest of Europe's giant mountains'. The gate to the High Tatras is considered to be the town of Poprad. It was probably established before the Tatar invasion, but the first written record of it comes only from 1256, when it consisted of two mutually independent villages: Poprad and Nemecká Ves, which merged towards the end of the 19th century. In 1412, Poprad (together with other Spiš towns) was pawned to Poland, and only in 1772 it was returned. It needs to be pointed out that Poprad in the past was always legging behind other towns in the region, and there was nothing in which it could compete with them. The real development of the town began only after the railway was built here in 1871. The city was finally linked with the villages and towns around, and following the mergers with many of them, Poprad is the biggest city in the vicinity of the High Tatras today. A legend has it that in the area of nowadays Poprad, amid the woods, used to stand a place for hermits – the Chapel of St. Egidius, which actually was a remainder of original monastery ruined by Tatars. Today, a Gothic-styled Church of St. Egidius from the 13th century belongs among the most significant sacral sights in the city. The church includes wall paintings coming from the first half of the 15th century. The

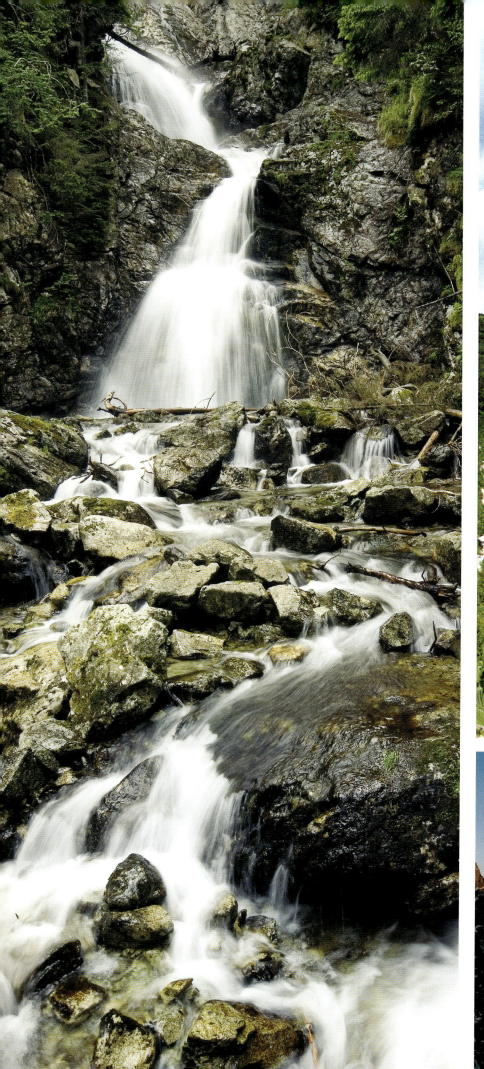

painting seen on the triumphal arch here is the oldest existing painting of the High Tatras skyline. Its author used the panorama of the peaks to make up a Bible scene of Christ's Resurrection.

On the square in Poprad, not far from the church, stands the building of Sub-Tatras Museum (in Slovak: Podtatranské múzeum), established already in 1886 as one of the first museums in Slovakia at all. This was thanks to a great admirer of the Tatras, David Husz, who also founded the first base for hikers in Poprad. In the town's borough of Veľká, several old townsmen's houses have been kept, plus an old Gothic Church of St. John the Evangelist, which dates back to the 13th century.

In the vicinity of Poprad, there is a couple of villages that also have interesting sites to of-fer. In the village of Stráže pod Tatrami we can visit an interesting Baroque garner from the 17th century, an originally-Gothic Roman-Catholic church from the 14th century which includes a well-preserved tower and walls, and which was later rebuilt into an Evangelical church in a Baroque style. Another village, Matejovce, offers us to see the Church of St. Stephen the King, which was built in the 14th century and is famous for its precious Gothic altar covered by paintings by a man whose name is known to every art lover around the world – Master of Matejovce. His paintings are interesting mainly thanks to his innovative approach, often described as late-Gothic Realism. Matejovce's Master has also paintings to see in churches in the towns of Levoča, Košice and Bardejov.

◄ The largest waterfall in the Tatras
  – Kmeťov vodopád
▲ Roháčske Tarn
▼ Yellow Tower and Prostredný Hrot Hills

NEXT PAGE
Malá Studená Dolina (valley)

PREŠOV

Athens upon Torysa

The metropolis of the Šariš area, nowadays the third largest city in Slovakia, Prešov, was given this apt name in the second half of the 17th century when an Evangelical collegium was established here to have a 'reforming' influence on the locals. Teachers, who usually came here after having graduated from German universities, disseminated the ideas of the Reformation. It was them who began to work on the tradition of education in Prešov. Building of the Evangelical collegium – today a national cultural monument – took 18 months and the construction works were financed by gifts by sponsors and money collected from common people. The collegium was soon known for an excellent level of its education system, employing well-known teachers, philosophers, theologians and writers from all around the Hungarian Empire, and even from abroad. Among its students were, for example, Imrich Thököly (an anti-Hapsburg resistance leader) and Jacob Bogdam, a famous English painter. During several uprisings of the Estates, various owners were in charge of the collegium, which was even a Jesuit residence for a certain period. Eventually, thanks to Emperor Joseph II, the institution reverted back to its original owner. Today, the building is the seat of the East District Bishop's Office of the Evangelical-Augsburg confession.

Establishment of educational institutions in Prešov was the result of a long historical process, the beginnings of which date as far back as 1247, when Prešov was first time mentioned in written documents. Prešov was granted the town privileges in 1299, and in 1324 it became a free royal town. First significant inhabiting of this area took place in mid and late stages of the Bronze Age. Slavic settlements, much later, were established here too and eventually became part of the Great Moravian Empire. With frequent invasions of Hungarian military groups, ethnic-Hungarian people arrived in Prešov to settle down at the turn of the 11th and the 12th centuries. Hungarian newcomers eventually formed an individual settlement near the Slavic one. Thanks to the town's geographical location, as well as flourishing

economy, developed settlements and King Belo IV visiting, German-Saxon colonists settled here in the early 13th century. The oldest existing written record of these times is the document dated November 7, 1247, which is a response by King Belo IV to a complaint raised by Cistercit monks from the town of Bardejov, accusing Prešov-based Germans of removing border signs from the monks' lands. In another preserved document, a letter from 1248, the king granted Germans lands. Later, in 1299, King Andrew III presented them with further rights, which made them fully integrated within the town. In 1342, Prešov was taken out of the administration by Šariš governance, which caused the town's self-governing position to improve. More than a century later, in 1480, Prešov became a member of so-called Pentapolitana – the association of five towns in the east of Slovakia.

The very early 15th century was marked by war against Turks, and during this period the town was pawned to several representatives of rich aristocracy. Prešov experienced rapid de-

velopment and lively building activities as of the second half of the 15th century, and it was in the course of the 16th century that the town gained the look very similar to how we know it today. At any rate, like elsewhere in Europe, the 16th and the 17th centuries brought a number of negatives to the town, including natural disasters, plague and uprisings. Prešov paid dearly especially for taking part in the uprising led by reformist Imrich Thököly. Following the unsuccessful attempt, the Imperial army captured the town, and the consequences were cruel. Besides being charged financially, Imperial General Caraffa condemned 24 Evangelical townsmen and local aristocrats to death. Although the town slowly began to grow afterwards, it was only as late as in the second half of the 18th century that Prešov could feel the comeback of economic wealth, along with social and cultural development. Except for the natural relief that the war is over, the end of WWI brought some uncertainties for Prešov. The town was a direct witness to an attempt to establish a Communist

LEFT PAGE
▲ Manuscript by Jonáš Záborský
◄ Former Rákoczi Palace, today seat of the Geographical Museum
► Monumental Church of St. Nicholas

RIGHT PAGE
◄ Memorial to Caraffa's Bloody Court
► Former Town Hall
▼ Solivar (saltworks)

Pavol Szinyei Merse (1845 – 1920), painter
Pavol Orszägh Hviezdoslav (1849 – 1921), the greatest poet in Slovakia's literary history
Koloman Banšell (1850 – 1887), poet, fiction writer and publicist
Teodor Zemplényi (1864 – 1917), painter
Koloman Hažlinský (1868 – 1907), painter
Július Sálandy (1868 – 1953), painter
Mikuláš Moyzes (1872 – 1944), composer, teacher
Jozef Gregor Tajovský (1874 – 1940), one of the best Slovak fiction writers and dramatists ever
Ernest Rákosi (1881 – 1973), painter

Mikuláš Jordán (1892 – 1977), painter
Leopold Lahola (1918 – 1968), fiction writer, filmmaker
The plate fixed on the wall of the building of a former Evangelical Collegium reads that Prešov was visited by 'the teacher of the nations' Jan Amos Comenius (1592 – 1670).
Prešov's lyceum was an employer of Ján Bocatius (1569 – 1621), a well-known poet of European importance, writing in Latin and German.

Places and sights worth visiting
Alexander Nevský's Temple

Cathedral of St. John the Baptist
Church of St. Nicholas
Church of the Holy Trinity
Fountain of Neptune
Geographical Museum
Jonáš Záborský Theatre
Klobušický Palace
Rákóczi Palace
Solivar
Wine Museum
Župný House

state, inspired by the Bolshevik Revolution in Russia. On June 16, 1919, the Slovak Republic of Councils (lasting only three weeks) was declared from here. Prešov's position became significantly stronger in the course of WWII, as it took much of the agenda previously belonging to the city of Košice, because Košice was in those times taken over by Hungary.

Among the best known sights in Prešov is definitely the Roman Catholic Church of St. Nicholas, which was built in the mid-14th century. Especially valuable sacral work of art in it is the main altar, which on its front side features sculptures of angels made by Master Paul of Levoča in the early 16th century. Master Paul is also author of the sculpture of crucified Christ, which we can admire in the church. On the square between the parish Church of St. Nicholas and the former Evanjelical Collegium building, you can find an Evangelic Church of the Holy Trinity, which comes from the mid-17th century. On the other hand, the Town Hall building dates back to the 16th century and underwent an extensive Classicist restoration in 1780. Initially, the building was used as a wine bar, and hence

you can find there a private wine museum today. Another museum, the geographical one, which includes a unique exposition devoted to the history of fire fighting in Slovakia, can be found in Rákóczi Palace, which stands near the parish church. It came into existence in the 16th century, following the reconstruction of older town houses, turning them into a representative seat of Sigmund Rákóczi. The top gem among the buildings on the southern end of Hlavná (Main) Street is the Greco-Catholic Cathedral of St. John the Baptist, which comes from the 18th century and is part of Greco-Catholic Bishop's Palace, as well as a part of Greco-Catholic Theological Faculty. The church was promoted to a cathedral after the Greco-Catholic bishopric was established in Prešov in 1981. The Franciscan monastery and church (in Gothic style) are also worth seeing. And talking about interesting sights in Prešov, we shouldn't omit Caraffa's House, built in 1624, which used to be the town's prison in the past. The last item on our list of remarkable sights in Prešov is the Jewish Orthodox Synagogue (built in 1898), where we can admire a collection of Judaic objects.

LEFT PAGE
▲ Fountain of Neptune on the square
▼ One of the most beautiful synagogues in Slovakia

RIGHT PAGE
◄ Church of St. Nicholas
► Burgher houses in the downtown have kept their original architecture.
▼ Hviezdoslav's Library

REVÚCA

Ancient Treasures

Some areas and regions are difficult to localise precisely, but it's easy with Gemer area. This part of Slovakia borders the national parks Slovenský raj (Slovak Paradise) and Muránska planina (Muráň Plateau), and is fringed by the protected nature area Slovenský kras (Slovak Karst) from the south side.

When depicting Gemer in detail, there's no need to be stingy with superlatives - this is a mountainous area with a lot of thick forests, wild and meandering streams, sheer mountain meadows, but also welcoming hillocks and bountiful fields with sky-blue surfaces of lakes and ponds. In addition, Gemer is an area of valleys and dells, where we can find many ancient sights - church-

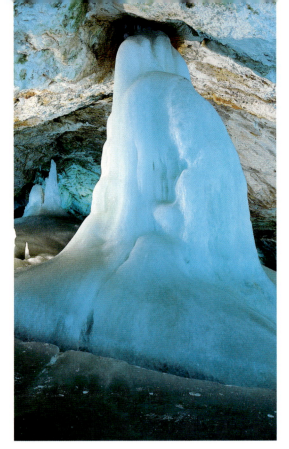

es, castles, manors, curia and well-preserved folk architecture.

The western part of Gemer, where among other towns Revúca lies, was one of the centres of Slovak national culture in the latter half of the 19th century. On September 19, 1862, the Slovak Evangelical Grammar School was founded here - known as the first secondary school in the history of Slovaks where the language of instruction was Slovak. A number of intellectual personalities of the nation taught here, such as Štefan Marko Daxner, Ján Francisci, Július Botto, Samuel Ormis, August Horislav Škultéty, Ivan Branislav Zoch and many more.

Nowadays in Revúca we can admire the original building of the first Slovak grammar

Important milestones in the area's history
1271 – first written record on the Muráň Castle
1357 – oldest written record on Revúca
1702 – Muráň Castle was hit by an extensive fire
1862 – Slovak Evangelical Grammar School was founded in Revúca
1867 – first financial association in Hungary was established here

1870 – Dobšina Ice Cave was discovered
1874 – grammar school in Revúca was forced to shut down

Famous personalities
Samuel Reuss (1783 – 1852), historian, ethnographer
Samuel Tomášik (1813 – 1887), poet, writer
Gustáv Reuss (1818 – 1861, botanist, historian, ethnographer
August Horislav Škultéty (1819 – 1892), patriotic awakener
Štefan Marko Daxner (1822 – 1892), publicist, lawyer
Ján Francisci (1822 – 1905), writer, translator
Samuel Ormis (1824 – 1875), teacher
Ivan Branislav Zoch (1843 – 1921), polymath
Július Botto (1848 – 1926), historian
Andrej Sokolik (1849 – 1912), cultural awakener

Places and sights worth visiting
Classicist Evangelical Church in Jelšava
Classicist Evangelical Church of Tolerance
  in Revúca
Coburgs' manor house in Jelšava
Dobšina Ice Cave
Muráň Castle
Muráň Plateau National Park
Roman-Catholic Church of St. Peter and Paul
  the Apostles in Jelšava
Roman-Catholic Church of St. Vavrinec the Deacon
  in Revúca
Slovak Evangelical Grammar School building
  in Revúca

school, a Rococco-styled curia from the 18th century. It's a national cultural sight, and a permanent historical exposition is installed inside. Besides this, there's a newer building of the first 'Slovak' grammar school (where Slovak was the language of instruction), built during 1871 – 1873 (period of growing repression towards the Slovak nation within the Austro-Hungarian Empire) from the money collected by the Slovak nation. A Roman-Catholic (late Gothic) Church of St. Vavrinec the Deacon and the Evangelical (Classicist) Church of Tolerance line the town's square.

Remains of the ruined Muráň Castle bear witness to rich and dramatic history of Gemer. The castle was historically important especially in the late 15th century when it belonged to the Jiskra Brotherhood. In the early 16th century it was conquered and captured by three marauding knights – Martin, Demeter and Matúš. But its main historic significance was during the era of anti-Hapsburg uprisings in the 17th century, when it became the centre of an uprising led by Count Wesselényi and the place where he romantically fell in love with Mária Széchyová, known as 'Muránska Venuša' (Venus of Muráň). Also the place where he conspired with her (to agree on how to capture the castle) in 1644 or 1645 is fabled even nowadays and known as Mária Széchyová's Spring. Mária fell in love with him, and she cooked up a plan that resulted in Count Wesselényi taking control of the castle. Muráň's ruins later brought bad luck to the count, as the uprising didn't work out well, and 'Venus' also met an untoward end. Mária spent a long time in prison for taking part in Wesselényi's conspiracy, and only death saved her from her suffering in the prison.

In those days the castle was in a blaze of glory, flourishing. However, following the fire in 1702, it slowly but steadily went in-

to decline. Its last owners, the Kohárys and Coburgs, were living in more comfortable seats in Jelšava and Svätý Anton respectively, instead. Ferdinand Coburg, former Bulgarian tsar, launched the construction of a shooting manor in the village of Predná Hora at the beginning of the 20th century. He couldn't finish the neo-Baroque manor because he died. After WWII, it was rebuilt into a sanatorium. Today, the romantic building is used as an absolutely unromantic site – the sanatorium is a last refuge for alcoholics and drug addicts.

The rich and noble family the Coburgs in the 16th century also owned another manor house in centre of a nearby town of Jelšava. They decided to have the Jelšava manor rebuilt into a Classicist seat. The reconstruction works were carried out between 1796 and 1801. Originally, a monastery from the 13th century used to stand in Jelšava, but the family commanded to bring it down and built a castle there, instead. Of the sacral sights in what was once a mining town, two Classicist-styled churches are dominant – Evangelical Church and Roman-Catholic Church of St. Peter and Paul the Apostles.

When looking for both historical sights and natural beauties in Gemer, you'd better go a little northward, where you'll find a unique natural creation, one of the most precious and most remarkable gems of nature in Slovakia. It's the Dobšina Ice Cave (in Slovak: Dobšinská ľadová jaskyňa), which ranks among the biggest ice caves in Europe with its length of 1 232 metres and depth of 112 metres, plus the entrance located 971 metres above sea level. Its uniqueness lies also in the fact that the cave contains more than 110,000 cubic metres of ice, which is in some passages thicker than 25 metres. Apart from the Alps, you cannot find such an icy spot anywhere in Europe.

LEFT PAGE
▲ Splendid and unique Dobšinská Ice Cave
▼ Slovak Evangelic Grammar School
– national cultural monument

RIGHT PAGE
▲ Breathtaking beauty of Muráň Plateau
▼ Burgher houses in the Jelšava

133

ROŽŇAVA

Medieval Glory of the Town and Castles Around

Rambling around Slovakia, you will find castles almost everywhere. Unfortunately, all that is left of many of them is ruins. Castles are slowly disappearing, along with pieces of history fading away... On a lonely hill in the east of the Gemer area, not far from the town of Rožňava, lies a castle which has luckily survived, and now represents a well-preserved dominant of the area - Krásna Hôrka Castle. It was built on an important medieval trade route that led to wealthy mining areas in Slovakia, namely the mountain range called Slovenské rudohorie. The castle's good fortune was largely influenced by one particular historical coincidence: during the well-known Battle of Slaná in 1241, it provided King Belo IV shelter from the Tatars. The thankful king gave his co-belligerents, the Bebek family, a number of extensive lands in the areas of Gemer and Turiec. Later, in 1318, the castle became the family's property for the next more than 300 years. There are several legends related to the rule of the family at the castle. Perhaps the best known is the story about the cruelty and insincerity of the castle's owner František Bebek and his brother Imrich, who was a regional governor in Gemer. The legend depicts the Bebeks as 'bur-

glarious knights' who used to pull church bells down to smelt them down into cannons. Thanks to this in Krásna Hôrka as well as in another castle nearby, Betliar, the biggest collection of original bronze cannons in Slovakia is proudly on offer. The upper wing of Krásna Hôrka includes a room that used to be a secret mint. Later on, the castle went under the administration of the Imperial court, which was administrating it via so-called 'castle captains'. This was when the Andrássy family, typical squires who were known for nurturing a wealthy feudal family tree, began their rule at the castle, which lasted nearly 400 years.

Throughout the following centuries, the castle was changing according to the needs of its residents, and in the 17th century it was extended in the spirit of late-Renaissance noble chateaux, which are believed to have been used purely for representation purposes. This is when Krásna Hôrka became the central seat of the region. In 1883 the Andrássys hosted here an exceptional personality - writer Mór Jókai, author of historical novels. Of course, no one could have predicted that his later novel 'Levočská biela pani' (White Lady of Levoča) would not only make the town of Levoča but also Krásna Hôrka Castle famous. The author created a legend that still lives within the castle's walls, and many visitors come to see 'the Krásna Hôrka Lady' Žofia Serédy, who rests in peace in a hyaloid sarcophagus. Some visitors come here to see whether the Lady has her right hand arisen - the hand that she meant to use to stave off patricide, as the legend has it.

At the turn of the 17th and the 18th century, the Andrássy brothers Stephen I (Štefan) and George II (Juraj) split up the family's properties, Stephen moved to Betliar and Juraj stayed in Krásna Hôrka. The next extensive rebuilding of Krásna Hôrka was later carried out under the command of Stephen III, and a splendid chapel

Important milestones in the town's history
1291 - the first document relating to the town
1418 - King Sigmund confirmed the town rights for Rožňava
1555 - town was captured by Turks

1711 - extensive fire devastated almost all the houses in the centre of the town
1776 - Empress Maria Theresé established bishopric in Rožňava

Famous personalities
Ján Szilassy (1705 - 1782), goldsmith
Andrej Jaslinský (1715 - 1784), physicist
Pavol Jozef Šafárik (1795 - 1861), writer
Jonáš Záborský (1812 - 1876), writer
Samuel Tomášik (1813 - 1887), writer
Samo Vozár (1823 - 1850), writer
Ľudovít Kubáni (1830 - 1869), writer
Samuel Ormis (1853 - 1855), collector, teacher

Július Tichý (1879 - 1920), painter
Koloman Tichý (1888 - 1968), painter

Places and sights worth visiting
Around Rožňava:
Betliar Castle
Count Andrássy's Gallery in Krásnohorské Podhradie
Krásna Hôrka Castle
In Rožňava:
Evangelical church
Franciscan Church of St. Ann
Roman-Catholic Church of the Assumption
Roman-Catholic Church of St. František Xaverský

was annexed to the castle, in which we can find an altar painting that features the Black Madonna of Krásna Hôrka, the patroness of the Andrássys. However, even the patroness couldn't protect the family completely, and as they felt uncomfortable in the castle, they left it at the dawning of the 19th century. When a clap of thunder hit the castle in 1817, causing an extensive fire and the castle burnt down, then-owner Countess Mária Andrássy-Festetich decided to have it restored. Her son George IV set up the Andrássy family museum at the castle, and his son, Count Dionýz, had the castle restored later on, again. In addition, Dionýz had a burial chamber built there. After his beloved wife Františka Hablowec died, a piety museum was established at the castle, too. It contains well-preserved and valuable applied-art objects coming from the previous three centuries.

Let's take a walk to Betliar Castle, which the Andrássys owned until 1945. During a reconstruction of the castle, probably in the spirit of Rousseau's slogan 'back to nature', a gorgeous English park was built around it that is one of a kind in Slovakia, made even more distinctive by the garden sculptures made of metal. Similar romantic decorations can be seen in the castle and its environs. Since its last rebuild, the castle has been, and still is, used as a sumptuous accommodation facility, providing services for well-to-do guests coming here for various social events, but mostly for hunts tak-

ing place in the nearby woods. Leopold Andrássy, another of the castle's owners, set up a big library here that contains many valuable publications. Restoration of the castle was professionally granted a prestigious European award 'Europa Nostra' in 1994.

Seemingly, but only at a first glance, the town of Rožňava rests in the shadow of these two lovely historical sites (Krásna Hôrka and Betliar castles). It's not quite so. The town also has much to show. It offers a number of admirable historical sights, incredibly fitting the lovely natural scenery surrounding it. Rožňava, a mining and bishopric town, spreads on a broad valley along the Slaná River, under the massif of the highest hill in Slovenské rudohorie – Volovec. The town became famous for mining gold, silver, copper, and later also iron ore. Alongside, Rožňava was an important centre of spiritual life – Hungarian Empress Maria Theresé established a bishopric here in 1775, and later the town was famous for its educational institutions, of which an Evangelical lyceum was the best known. Rožňava's dominant sight is a Gothic Cathedral of the Assumption, a Jesuit Church of St. František Xaverský, a Franciscan Church of St. Ann, plus we can find here an Evangelical and a Lutheran church. Also in the town, we can admire a white memorial to the patroness of the poor Františka Andrássyová, built in Secession style.

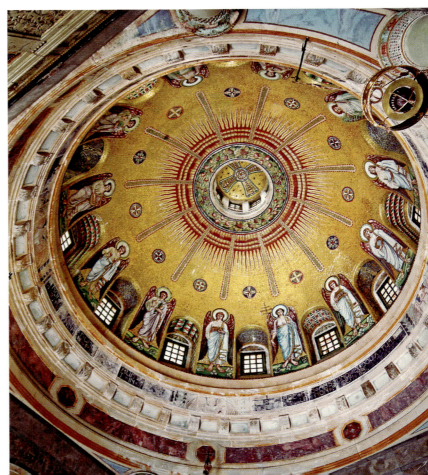

SABINOV

Medieval Glory in the Shadow

When filmmakers came to Sabinov in the summer of 1965, they certainly didn't even think about the fame which was to came later for this district town located in northern part of the Spiš area with the release of the film 'Shop on the Main Street'. The producers, the staff and the actors occupied the main square in the town for only a few weeks, but the on-screen result impressed people and critics all around the world, making Sabinov and Slovakia (or, Czechoslovakia then) known worldwide. Today, we know that the film directors Ján Kádar and Elmar Klos intentionally chose Sabinov to be the setting for the tragic story featuring the times of the Slovak State (a Nazi-modeled independent state, lasting from March 14, 1939 to April 1945) for good reason. It was during this time that the confiscation of Jewish properties was carried out, and the people of Sabinov experienced these times first-hand. Sabinov had many Jewish citizens during WWII, all of whom were taken to concentration camps and only a few of them survived to come back home. The film's both outdoor and indoor sequences were shot in the town, and many people remember the unforgettable and excellent Slovak actor Jozef Króner in the leading role. One year after the film was shot it received the top movie prize - an Oscar. These Oscar memories are still alive, and nowadays in the town we can find a store bearing the title of the film.

This special event was, at least for a while, a pleasant change to the everyday, stereotyped life of Sabinov, given that the splendid little town had been for years living in the shadow of the Spiš region's centre, the much larger city of Prešov. Nonetheless, Sabinov has been always breathing with a medieval, almost forgotten beauty. It's enough to take a walk in the centre of the town, through the square and its side streets to realise this. The ancient bastions and the town walls are the best proof of Sabinov's past glory. The spirit of the past cannot be erased, and the town chronicle also contains enough to whet the appetite of history buffs. As we open it and read its pages, we discover that the first

LEFT PAGE
▲ The church's portal
◄ Church of St. John the Baptist Being Cut
► Municipal Office building

RIGHT PAGE
◄ Interior of the church, including Gothic carvings from the workshop of Master Paul
► Sculpture of St. John the Apostle inside church

Important milestones in the town's history
1248 - the first written record of Sabinov, referred to as a 'royal village'

1299 - the town was granted the so-called Spiš Rights
1405 - Sabinov was promoted to a free royal town
1461 - local church was set on fire
1530 - lyceum was found in Sabinov

Famous personalities
Samuel Fáry (1769 - 1826), poet
Bohuslav Nosák-Nezabudov (1818 - 1877), poet
Ján Cuker (1828 - 1890), poet
Jolana Cirbusová (1884 - 1940), writer

Janko Borodáč (1892 - 1964), actor, director
Anton Pridavok (1904 - 1945), poet, writer, publicist

Places and sights worth visiting
Building of a former lyceum
Church of St. John the Baptist Being Cut
Former town walls

The town is a starting-out point for a recreational area called Drienica-Lysá, with excellent conditions for downhill skiing.

record of the town comes from 1248, when Sabinov is mentioned to be a developed royal village.

The next important milestone in the town's history was 1299, when it (along with Prešov and Veľký Šariš) was granted the so-called Spiš Rights by Hungarian King Andrew III. The set of rights included the right to elect a mayor and a vicar, the right to establish a court, hunting and fishing rights, tax and custom exemptions, as well as relaxed conditions for military service duties. This legal act made Sabinov a town, in fact. Another set of privileges was granted to the town in 1405, promoting Sabinov to a free royal town. The town became a member of Pentopolitana, an association of five eastern-Slovak towns that also included Košice, Prešov, Bardejov and Levoča in the late 15th century.

Sabinov flourished the most between the 16th and 18th centuries. This was the period of building several dominant sights in the town. Unfortunately, the 19th century brought here an economic, political and social decline, and Sabinov turned into nothing but a small provincial town. Over the Restoration period it was known for its education institutions, including the quite progressive Piarist grammar school founded in 1740. During the era of the first Czechoslovak Republic the town had its own sawmill, tannery and cannery, which provided jobs for many of the locals, while others were engaged chiefly in farming.

The oldest and the most significant architectonic sight in Sabinov is a Gothic Church of St. John the Baptist Being Cut, which dates back to the 14th century. The original church was almost completely burnt in 1461, during a fire so extensive that even the church bells were nearly dissolved. The church was rebuilt between 1484 and 1518, and nowadays we can admire its Gothic, Renaissance and Baroque features. The most precious item inside the church was the main altar, carved by famous Master Paul of Levoča. The church only has a copy of it now, as the original can be seen in the Hungarian National Museum in Budapest.

There's another architectonic highlight in the town – the building of a former lyceum, built in 1530, which was later adapted towards the needs of Piarist grammar school. Sabinov also has a Greco-Catholic church, two Evangelical churches and an Orthodox temple. As has been mentioned above, we can admire the remains of the town walls here, with eight out of the original 13 bastions still standing.

Sabinov also used to hold various cultural and social events, with a number of groups and organizations involved. For example, a local theatre group Palárik was successful here between 1922 and 1924. Life in the town was marked by the recession in the early 20th century, followed by another disaster – the Second World War. Even though enormities of the war affected the locals badly, after the liberation the town recovered rapidly, building new plants and factories piecemeal, and this small town (population some 3,000) grew into a modern town with about 12,000 citizens. Today, Sabinov is the second largest town in Prešov region.

SPIŠSKÁ NOVÁ VES

The Town of Streets of the Sun

In Spišská Nová Ves, the centre of southern Spiš, near the main square, we can find two streets with simple names – one is called Letná (Summer) Street, and the other is Zimná (Winter) Street.

It wouldn't be unusual had they not been given names according to their real locations. While Zimná Street is all year long cooled by the shadows of the facades of the town houses turned northwards, Letná Street is on sunny days warmed by rays of the sun. Local people are well used to this natural phenomenon, but visitors are unlikely to notice it at all, as they're usually captured by other interesting things that the town offers.

And there's one more singularity in Spišská Nová Ves – the town was being built along the road, which resulted in houses having very narrow allotments, and which in turn meant the large square had a lenticular shape like a spindle. The square itself is, the largest of all squares in the region. The dominant feature of the square is Church of the Assumption, built in the second half of the 14th century where an older church used to stand in the 13th century. In 1395, Gothic Chapel of St. Michael was added to the church. The chapel is still standing, and is relatively well-preserved. Later, alike others around, the church went through several restorations which affected the way it looks now. Especially its tower is impressive, with the height of 86 metres being the highest church tower in Slovakia. The church's interior is decorated in both Gothic and Renaissance spirit, looking majestic and genteel – thanks to hands of old masters having touched it. What's indeed interesting inside the church is the Calvary carving – a late-Gothic work by Master Paul of Levoča, but also Gothic panel paintings of the Virgin Mary. Classical pews, carved by T. Thern in 1797, have also been preserved in the church.

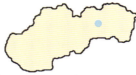

Important milestones in the town's history
1271 – King Stephen V granted (German-)Saxons living in Spiš area a privilege, which recognised their right to self-govern
1317 – the right for Saxons to govern over themselves was confirmed and modified by ruler Charles Robert
1481 – the oldest existing record of the town's school

Famous personalities
Karol Juraj Rumy (1780 – 1847), polymath
Jozef Hanula (1863 – 1944), painter
Ernest Rákoši (1881 – 1973), painter
Ervin Lazar (1905 – 1988), literary scientist, teacher
Mikuláš Huba (1919 – 1986), actor, teacher

Places and sights worth visiting
Evangelical church
Gothic church and chapel in Spišský Štrvtok
Manor house in Betlanovce
Markušovce Castle
Monastery (in Slovak referred to as 'Kláštorisko') near Letanovce
Province House
Town Hall
Town houses on Letná and Zimná Street
Reduta

Between 1790 and 1796, an Evangelical church was built, completely in Classicist style. Inside, visitors can see an impressive altar painting by J. J. Stunder, from 1797, that features Jesus on Olive Mountain.

Another interesting building in the town is Reduta – the most significant Secession site in Slovakia. It was built between 1900 and 1905, based on the project by architect K. Gerster. In the present, it's a seat of the Spiš Theatre. The building draws our attention at the first glance – with its four towers on the roof. When walking in the streets of Spišská Nová Ves, you can't miss out some town houses, markedly influenced by Gothic and Renaissance, which can be seen mainly on the vaults, portals and window. The boldest of these houses is a one-storey building – former headquarters of the Association of 16 Spiš Towns – so-called Province House, now the seat of Geographical Museum.

Sightseers in Spišská Nová Ves surely won't resist the surroundings, because there's much to see around, too. Taking it westwards from the town, you'll go through several villages entering the gate to the Slovenský Raj (Slovak Paradise) National Park. This is where the real paradise opens up for you – natural miracles including gauges, waterfalls and caves. The earthly treasures of ancient Spiš area only make up the unforgettable atmosphere, which you can breathe only in a few places in Slovakia.

For example, the village of Spišský Štvrtok is worth checking out. It's the place lying on the junction of historically important roads. Nearby, but still belonging to the village, in the place called Myšia Hôrka (literally 'Mouse Hill'), there's an archaeological area where findings coming from the times of the Otoman culture were dug out, and where the most beautiful Gothic chapel in Slovakia (built in 1473) stands. Archaeologists also found artefacts dating as far back as to the late Iron Age in the village of Hrabušice, where the most precious sight is an originally-Romanesque church from the mid-13th century, in which you can admire an extremely valuable item – a Gothic altar with wings. Built over the same historical period, Marcel Castle can be seen on the nearby the Zelená Hora ('Green Hill'), now standing only in ruins. Another village in the area, called Markušovce, which used to be a lookout village in the 12th century, became famous mainly thanks to a noble family – the Mariassys – who had a Renaissance manor house built in here.

Nearby, on a hillside rising from the basin of the Hornád River, you can find a unique rocky formation – Markušovský skalný hríb ('Markušovce's Rocky Mushroom'), while the ruined Markušovce Castle spreads above the village. The village of Letanovce also has a moved history, as it originally used to be a property of the Spiš Castle.

LEFT PAGE
◀ 'Province House' today houses Geographical Museum.
▶ Church of the Assumption, having the highest bell-tower in Slovakia

RIGHT PAGE
▲ Classicist building of Town Hall
▼ Renaissance chateau in Markušovce

SPIŠSKÉ PODHRADIE, SPIŠSKÁ KAPITULA AND SPIŠ CASTLE

Divine Gift and Royal Message

Important milestones in history of Spiš

1198 – ecclesiastical collegium was founded (later became regional chapter)
1209 – Spiš Castle mentioned as the seat of the Spiš region
1321 – Spišské Podhradie was granted town privileges
1382 – Corporis Christi chapel was annexed to the cathedral's southern wall and consecrated

1450 – the oldest record on municipal Latin school in Spišské Podhradie
1583 – fire in Spišské Podhradie
1950 – Spišská Kapitula announced to be a protected urban area
1993 – Spiš Castle and neighbouring sites were put on the list of World's Cultural Heritage by UNESCO

Famous personalities

Ján Bayer (1630 – 1674), philosopher, teacher
Štefan Mišik (1843 – 1919), historian, folklorist
Ján Vojtaššák (1877 – 1965), ecclesiastical dignitary
Ladislav Granč (born 1920), writer
Edmund Hleba (born 1926), literary historian, teacher

Places and sights worth visiting

In Spiš area:
Church of the Holy Spirit in the village of Žehra
Spiš Castle
In Spišská Kapitula:
Bishopric Palace
Chapel of the Zápoľský family
Clocktower
Sculpture of Ján Nepomucký the Saint
St. Martin Cathedral
In Spišské Podhradie:
Merciful Brothers monastery
Church of Our Lady
Church of St. John of God
Town Hall

Ancient and medieval towns, forts and castles are usually misty, steeped in legend, but Spiš area doesn't need legends. All it takes is to take a look around, and you'll feel like as if you're in a magical fairytale. You raise your head and look up to see the High Tatras beneath the vault of clouds; you tip your eyes down to see breathtaking nature all around. Under ground there are deposits of rare minerals, and above ground you admire many Gothic architectural gifts.

Today, a small province town of Spišské Podhradie lives its everyday life and quietly remembers the past glory. The town is from both sides watched by monuments of the past. From the traventine hillock, we get a lovely view of Spiš Castle, for centuries the seat of municipal authorities, while from the smaller hummock on the other side you can see the very small town of Spišská Kapitula (literally: the Spiš Chapter), which has always been the seat of spiritual authorities. In the centre of Spišská Kapitula, which is often called 'the Slovak Vatican', we can find Bishopric Cathedral, Bishopric Palace and the houses of canons. In 1198 Spišská Kapitula became the seat of collegium for the area of Spiš, and soon after also the headquarters of the regional chapter. Since 1776 it's been the seat of Spiš's bishopric. If you

deliberately want to get stuck in with the history of the town, it's enough to take a walk through Cannon Street (in Slovak: Ulica Kanonikov). Houses on the street have Baroque-styled decorations – sculptures, paintings and mosaics. Even original interior decorations have been preserved in some of them, and each has a smaller house hidden in the backyard, which used to be home to servants. At the end of the street you come up towards a clocktower built in Baroque style, dated 1739, which originally served as an entrance gate to the French park belonging to Bishopric Palace. Above the clocktower stands firmly, sculpted in the stone, the patron of the local ecclesiastical seminary – Ján Nepomucký the Saint. The dominant sight of Spišská Kapitula is St. Martin's Cathedral, which is by architects considered to be a textbook study of the development of Romanesque and Gothic architecture.

The town of Spišské Podhradie hasn't always been successfully protected by its patrons. Like Spišská Kapitula, it has a rich history, and experienced upswings and declines, but its citizens' lives have always been closely connected with Spiš Castle. Until WWII, the town lived on crafts to satisfy the needs of the castle, but perhaps the best reputation was enjoyed by the local producers

LEFT PAGE
Spiš Castle and Spišská Kapitula

RIGHT PAGE
▲ Altar of Our Lady in Spišská Kapitula
◄ Romanesque church in the village of Bijacovce
► Romanesque rotunda in Bijacovce

of sausages, who supplied even luxurious Budapest hotels with this delicacy. Due to good commercial conditions, a large Jewish community lived here in those pre-war days – the town was crossed by an important trade route, on which merchants' carriages used to meet to exchange goods.

German colonists came to the area of Spiš in the 12th century. Some of them settled down right next to the settlement round the castle. They built the Church of Our Lady and called their new settlement Kirchdorf. Along with Spišské Podhradie (with which it later merged), the colonist village was granted privilege by the Hungarian king in 1271 and became a small but free town. This brought the greatest economic and cultural boom in the town's history. But the good times ended in 1412, when Spišské Podhradie – together with another 16 towns of Spiš – was pawned to a Polish king. Luckily enough, Polish administrators respected the old rights of Spiš's citizens, thanks to

which the town could keep its distinctiveness. Visitors can nowadays admire beautiful bourgeoisie houses with big gates, as well as the aforementioned Church of Our Lady, the tower of which still has Romanesque features of the 13th century.

Rambling around the country beneath Spiš Castle, we shouldn't miss out the village of Žehra, which became famous almost worldwide thanks to its rare and ancient little church. The strange name of the village is often discussed – what exactly does it mean, actually? It could have been derived from the word 'žeh', which is an obsolete Slovak/Slavic word for 'burning'. The Slavic tribe from the nearby hill Drevenik are thought to have used the area of the nowadays Žehra as a cult gathering place where they used to burn dead human bodies. However, this is nothing but unsubstantiated theory, unlike the exact dating of the church. Historians say it was built from travertine rocks between 1245 and 1275.

LEFT PAGE
St. Martin's Cathedral in Spišská Kapitula

RIGHT PAGE
▲ Breathtaking ancient monument – Spiš Castle
▼ Church of the Holy Spirit in the village of Žehra

Now, let's have a walk on a meandering path that takes us towards Spiš Castle – one of the largest in central Europe – which was built in the 12th century on the area of former Slavic fortified settlement. Although it resisted the pressure of the Tatar army in 1242, later in the century masters from northern Italy were called to firm the castle walls. The castle's rounded tower and Romanesque palace both date back to the 13th century. The castle, originally a royal seat, belonged to a couple of noble families in the past – the Zápoľskýs, the Thurzos and the Čákis. The latter family left it in ruins. Fortunately, the authorities launched a conservation effort concerning the walls after WWII, and over the recent years the castle has un-

dergone comprehensive restoration – after archaeological research was carried out – in order to save it for the future. This is a positive trendline, because the castle walls are hiding an enduring royal message from the past, which deserves to be respected. That unique and magnifiscent view from the castle's tower, taking our eyes to the foothills of lovely High Tatras, is a gift we should be thankful for. Spiš Castle as a historical complex, together with some other neighbouring sites (Spišské Podhradie, Spišská Kapitula and Church of the Holy Spirit in the village of Žehra), was put on the list of World Heritage List by UNESCO in 1993. This proves that not only Slovakia, but also authorities abroad respect such gifts.

LEFT PAGE
Interior of the Church of the Holy Spirit

RIGHT PAGE
▲ Holy shrine, dated 1675, near the mineral spring at Sivá Brada

▼ White Lion inside St. Martin's Cathedral

STARÁ ĽUBOVŇA

Jewel in Nature

Roman Emperor Marcus Aurelisus noticed both the lovely nature and advantageous strategic location of the northern Spiš region, meaning around the district town of Stará Ľubovňa, and wanted to expand his empire's northern borders up to here.

However, the first inhabitants of the area had noticed it long before Marcus Aurelius. The oldest evidence of the area being populated is the archaeological finding – a greyish sedimentary rock from the Palaeolithic era. The oldest written record of Stará Ľubovňa dates back only to 1292, however. After the local castle was built, the original village turned into a settlement round the castle, and grew in importance. The next milestone in the town's history was 1364, when King Louis I granted it with two privileges. Firstly, it was promoted to a royal town having the same rights as the towns of Košice and Budín had been given before. The second privilege concerned the prestige to hold annual fairs. Another advantage for the town was

the fact that it was included in the group of sixteen Spiš towns that King Sigmund pawned to Poland (in those times called The Polish Crown), which was between 1412 and 1772. Stará Ľubovňa became the administrative centre of the pawned area during this period, and this contributed to its further growth and provided the town with many great development opportunities. The town took the chance and became a well-known economic and cultural centre for the whole region. Therefore, paradoxically, when the pawn was cancelled and the towns went back to the Hungarian Empire, Stará Ľubovňa lost a lot, including its privileged position among the towns of Spiš. The dominance, in these terms, was naturally shifted towards another town – Spišská Nová Ves.

The town's past prosperity and glory is reflected in the architecture of its historical core, which mostly consists of a rectangle-shaped square, called St. Nicholas Square, with bourgeois houses built in Renaissance

Important milestones in the town's history
1292 – the oldest written record of Stará Ľubovňa
after 1346 – St. Nicholas Square was built
1412 – peace treaty signing between Hungarian King Sigmund Luxembourg and Polish King Vladislav II took place at Ľubovňa Castle

1412 – Stará Ľubovňa was included in the group of 16 towns of Spiš
1557 – fire burst out at Ľubovňa Castle
1778 – 16 towns of Spiš formed so-called Province
1991 – Ľubovňa Castle's chapel was rebuilt and sanctified

Famous personalities
Pantaleon Jozef Roškovský (1734 –1789), Baroque poet
Ferdinand Vokál (1921), poet belonging to Catholic Modernism literary movement

Places and sights worth visiting
Church of St. Nicholas
Exposition of Folk Architecture (underneath Ľubovňa Castle)

Greco-Catholic Church of Mother the Helpful
Jewish Cemetery
Ľubovňa Castle
Old Cemetery
Province House
Roman-Catholic Church of St. Peter and St. Paul
Roman-Catholic St. Joseph's Church
St. Nicholas Square

style, which were later restored under the influence of Baroque and Classicism. The highlights of the square are the Church of St. Nicholas and Province House, a former seat of the governor of the pawned Spiš towns. The Renaissance arcade house standing on pillars was restored after it was torched in 1639, which involved the joining of two individual buildings.

The house was said to be a mysterious place, apparently. For example, people whispered that a recruit was immured in the basement hall. In order to confirm or deny this hearsay mystery, the rocky part of the wall was taken out in late 20th century. At the examination experts found an epitaph and a feature of part of a male figure inside.

Church of St. Nicholas comes from the end of the 13th century, and was rebuilt in the second half of the 17th century. In its interior we can see an extremely precious late-Gothic baptismal font. It was made of stone in the 16th century. Plus there are tombstones (also late Gothic) that are made of sandstone and red marble. Also inside the church, the side altars and a 'Grief over Christ' sculpture are very valuable. A large painting depicting St. Nicholas, painted in the second half of the 19th century, is worth mentioning, too.

The town has three more churches. St. Joseph's Church is located in the town part called Podsadek, and is interesting mainly for its bell tower built only in 1991, which replaced the old one made of wood in 1960s. The bell was brought from Ľubovňa Castle, where it had been installed until then. Greco-Catholic Church of Mother the Helpful was sanctified only recently, in 1993. Pope John Paul II consecrated its foundation stone during his visit to Slo-

vakia in 1990. The newest of all churches in the town is the Church of St. Peter and St. Paul, sanctified in 1999.

When talking about Stará Ľubovňa, we shouldn't omit Ľubovňa Castle, located in the vicinity of the town and built at the turn of the 13th and 14th centuries in order to watch over the Polish-Hungarian border. Queen Mary as well as Hungarian King Sigmund Luxembourg also visited the castle. Sigmund came here in 1412 to meet Polish ruler Vladislav II with an eye to signing a peace treaty between Hungary and Poland. Vladislav fell in love with the castle so much that he loaned Sigmund 37,000 ducats just to get the castle (plus other Spiš towns) as a pawn.

The castle was under Polish administration for four centuries, and when Swedes invaded Poland, the Polish coronation jewels were kept here. In 1553, the castle was on fire, and when it was subsequently restored, it was changed to a Renaissance palace/fortress. Another restoration took place in the 17th century, featuring the new gate, eastern bastion, early-Baroque palace and chapel. Following the end of Polish administration of Ľubovňa Castle and parts of Spiš region, in 1772 during the rule of Empress Maria Theresé, the castle lost its dominant and influential position.

After the renewal in 2003 the castle was opened for public, and the main tower belongs among the greatest of what it offers. The Museum of Folk Architecture is installed underneath the castle, containing a set of buildings collected from the villages around. This collection thus gives us an impression of visiting the original settlement that used to round the castle in the past.

LEFT PAGE
▲ Ľubovňa Castle
◄ Valuable relics kept inside Ľubovňa Castle
▼ A look inside Church of St. Nicholas in Stará Ľubovňa

RIGHT PAGE
▲▼ Ľubovňa Castle

SVIDNÍK

Pluses and Minuses of the Amber Route

Only an expert could give you an answer to what "svida" and "svib" are. An expert could playfully complement a Latin expression *Cornus sanquinea,* which refers to leafy vegetation. And this is exactly what the district town of Svidník in the east of Slovakia is named after. Svidník's roots go back to the prehistoric times. In the late Bronze Age and early Iron Age, there was a remarkable route leading through this area, along what we know now as the Topľa River. The existence of the route is proven by findings of various bronze objects.

In spite of the fact that the area was rich in precious archaeological objects all throughout history, it has always remained a poor piece of land. People here were living on pasturage and agriculture. In addition, the area was often stormed by military raids, plundered by bandits, and assailed by numerous natural disasters. Notwithstanding penury and poverty, hard times have always brought local people together, and poor inhabitants have thus always been united – with Slovaks, Ruthenians and Ukrainians for centuries living side by side, later also with Jewish, Roma and Polish.

In fact, there was no century without military raids penetrating the area in the past. People living around Svidník in the 15th century witnessed frequent invasions by Polish forces, and – as if this wasn't enough – the end of the century was marked by bandit inroads. One example is that of the bandit band of Fedor Holovatý, headquartered in Black Mountain, from where it made incursions into Zborov, Stropkov and Šariš castles. Bandits' secret tunnels, which could speak volumes about the bandit raids, can be seen under the southern side of the Black Mountain even today. Many past events can only be presumed now, but with a certain dose of logic it is possible to piece together a mysterious mosaic of the past here.

The medieval "path" of the Amber Route obviously crossed the area, however. It meandered along the Ondava River, near Stočin and Svidník, heading northeast through Ladomírová towards the border pass, continuing into Poland. It's difficult to say if it was more a good thing than a bad thing for people living here those days. Usually, everything has both pluses and minuses. A positive thing about the route coming through this area was the fact that Ladomírová had its own tollhouse and a chateau, and a tollgate in Stročin was built even earlier. This is what made both villages significantly richer, proof of which is

LEFT PAGE

▲ Icon from the wooden church in Miroľa
◀ Wooden church in the village of Miroľa
▶ Sculpture in the church in Miroľa

RIGHT PAGE

▲ Wooden church in Ladomírová
▼ A gospel-book in the church in Miroľa

Important milestones in the town's history
1434 – the first written record on Ruthenians in Svidník
1611 – record on school in the town

between 1715 and 1720 – after Rákóczi's uprisings the region became partially depopulated
1795 – local chateau was built
until 1849 – Svidník belonged to the Makovica domain, headquartered in Zborov Castle
1944 – Carpathian-Dukla Operation took place

Famous personalities
Ivan Polyvka, teacher
Alexander I. Pavlovič, poet and patriotic awakener of Ruthenians

Places and sights worth visiting
D. Milly Gallery
Dukla Museum
Korejovce, Nižný Komárnik, Vyšný Komárnik, Prikra, Bodruža, Miroľa and Potoky
Military Open-air Museum of Carpathian-Dukla Operation
Museum of Material and Spiritual Culture of Ukrainians and Ruthenians
Wooden little churches in the following villages: Dobroslava, Ladomírová, Šemetkovce, Krajné Čierno, Hunkovce

a golden coin from the times of King Matthias Corvinius found in Ladomírová. On the other hand, the region's military-strategic location negatively contributed to it being plundered during Hungarian-Polish wars. The armies were reluctant to stop for anything, and it was probably then that the fortified settlement at Kaštielinik burnt down and the village of Rusinec ceased to exist. Ravaging of the region continued in the following years, too. Joseph II, ruler during the Enlightenment Era, had a military road built here. The path is mentioned as Josephian Road in historical documents and, indeed, it was built for a reason – Russian troops were taking the road, moving down to northern Italy in the spring of 1799. Famous Cossack units were coming back to Russia this way in 1800, and in 1806 Russian army led by Commander Kutuzov used the road on the way home from the Battle of Austerlitz. In mid-19th century the road served as a way for the military troops of Austrian Marshal F. H. Schlick, Marshal Volg and Russian Archduke Constantine. A bad situation got even worse with the launch of the WWI, during which the villages in the region were ransacked and the town of Svidnik burnt down. Eventually, Svidnik became famous for perhaps the best known military operation of the WWII – Carpathian-Dukla Operation, which was originally meant to

help the guerrillas during the Slovak National Uprising in August 1944. Tough battles, escalated by severe frost, lasted until the end of January 1945, when the region was finally liberated. Nowadays, the Military Open-air Museum of Carpathian-Dukla Operation serves as site to remember the toughest collisions around the saddle back on the main ridge of the Low Beskyds – at the border pass to Poland.

Despite having been through trying times, people of the region have always lived very spiritually. Church schools existed here already in medieval times, and the region is especially known for a remarkable number of wooden little churches standing here. There were 330 of such churches all around Slovakia, of which only a fifth has been preserved until today, and as many as 13 of them you can found in the district of Svidnik. Given that the majority of the local people are Orthodox and Greco-Catholic faithful, churches of eastern rite have prevalence. They are characterised by triple towers, roofs with onion-shaped cupolas, and richly carved architectonic details. Interiors of these splendid little churches are exceptionally impressive, thanks to decorative paintings on the walls, wooden altars, and especially thanks to iconostasis that dominate here.

VRANOV NAD TOPĽOU

The Truth about the Book of Lies

'This land is rich. There's everything that people need for living. Stay here,' said a hermit to a merchant, as a legend has it. The hermit saved the merchant's life with the help of some crows, who warned him of a man fallen into an abyss. Eventually, the merchant stayed and built a house near the Topľa River, and some others followed him. In the years to come the place grew into a settlement, then a village, and later became a town. As houses were added, the name of the place was constantly changing. At first, the settlement was reportedly called Vrania, or Vranie. Later, when it became a town with brick houses, the name changed to Vranov (a variant of the previous ones, meaning something like 'a place of crows'). This is how legends have it, but the solid historical facts are much more sober, indicating that the first mention of the town comes from 1270. In the past, the town was the centre of the Čičva manor and developed as a serf town. The local Čičva Castle belonged to the manor as well - a gift from King Stephen V to a nobleman Rainold (in 1270) for his credits on royal military campaigns. His heirs owned the castle until 1523. Since then, it's been veiled under a cloak of mystery. In 1524 King Louis II granted the whole manor to the noble family of Báthorys. When the infamous Alžbeta Báthoryová (Elisabeth Bathory) married Franz Nádašdy in 1575, the wedding was held either in Vranov Castle or in Čičva Castle. The life story of the 'bloody countess' Báthory is well known, at least some parts of it. It's said that she wanted to keep her youth and beauty by taking baths in the blood of virgins, and between 1585 and 1610 the cruel countess allegedly tortured and killed hundreds of girls and young women in the castles belonging to her husband and relatives. So far, no evidence has been found as to whether these cruelties also took place in Čičva Castle. Let's get back to facts, which show that the castle used to hold sessions of Zemplín region starting in 1527. The castle played an important role in several anti-Hapsburg uprisings, and after Rákoczi's Uprising (1711) it was definitively destroyed, and since then it's been in ruins. Among the curiosities related

Church of St. Franz of Assisi
Čičva Castle
Monastery

Important milestones in the town's history
1310 – the oldest written record of the town
1314 – mention of a parish church here
1361 – Vranov granted a privilege to have a storehouse and hold fairs

1718 – conflagration in the town
1778 and 1779 – the town and its surroundings hit by earthquakes
1831 – Eastern Slovak Peasant Uprising took place
1948 – foundation stone for the pulp-mill and paper-mill laid in Hencovce
1991 – Andy Warhol's Museum of Modern Art opened in Medzilaborce

Places and sights worth visiting
Andy Warhol's Museum of Modern Art in Medzilaborce
Church of Nativity of Our Lady

◀ Church of Nativity of Our Lady

▶ Unusual interior of the church

to the castle's history is the so-called 'Book of Lies and Liars', which was kept at the castle and in which various lies were recorded, together with the names of liars. The book was well known all around Slovakia as the Čičva Book. Vranov nad Topľou is recorded in infamy in the books of Slovak history for the Eastern Slovak Peasant Uprising that took place here in 1831, and which belongs among the most dramatic events of the first half of the 19th century.

The region's economic development was dominated by agricultural production in the following years. In terms of its modern economic development, important milestones for the town and district were May 16, 1948, when the foundation stone for the pulp and paper mill was laid in the village of Hencovce, and September 1, 1955, when production was launched there.

Like other former serf towns, Vranov nad Topľou held only a few artistic and historical monuments and sights. These towns lacked rich citizens and bourgeoisie, who would potentially support and sponsor construction activities. Due to this, such towns cannot even compare to free royal towns, for example. When it comes to Vranov nad Topľou, the highest proportion of credits on construction of representation buildings must be given to feudal noblemen and the church. The highlight among the town's sacral sights is

Roman Catholic Church of Nativity of Our Lady, which was built in 1580. Especially its interior is valuable as it hides a precious set of golden silver objects made by well-known goldsmith Ján Szillasy from Levoča. The set consists of a monstrance and a chalice, and is treated with belaboured and enamelled decor. In the 17th century, a Baroque monastery was built as a complement to the church on the northern side. Other noticeable sacral sights include a Roman Catholic Church of St. Franz of Assisi, a pseudo-Gothic evangelical church, and a Greco-Catholic church.

Vranov nad Topľou district, but in particular the small town of Medzilaborce and the little village of Miková near the Polish border, became world famous due to pop-art king Andy Warhol's parents coming from here. Andy Warhol's Museum of Modern Art was established in Medzilaborce in 1991. Here, visitors have a unique chance to admire works and authentic objects from Warhol's life from an artistically original perspective – space as part of a painting. This is achieved by the fact that the works are installed in continuity with papered walls, creating an impression of a single visual unit. Although Andy Warhol never even visited his parents' birthplace, and knew it only from his mother's recollections, Medzilaborce is a town renowned as a result of the continued global fascination with Warhol.

▲ Čičva Castle in ruins

▼ Wall painting inside the church

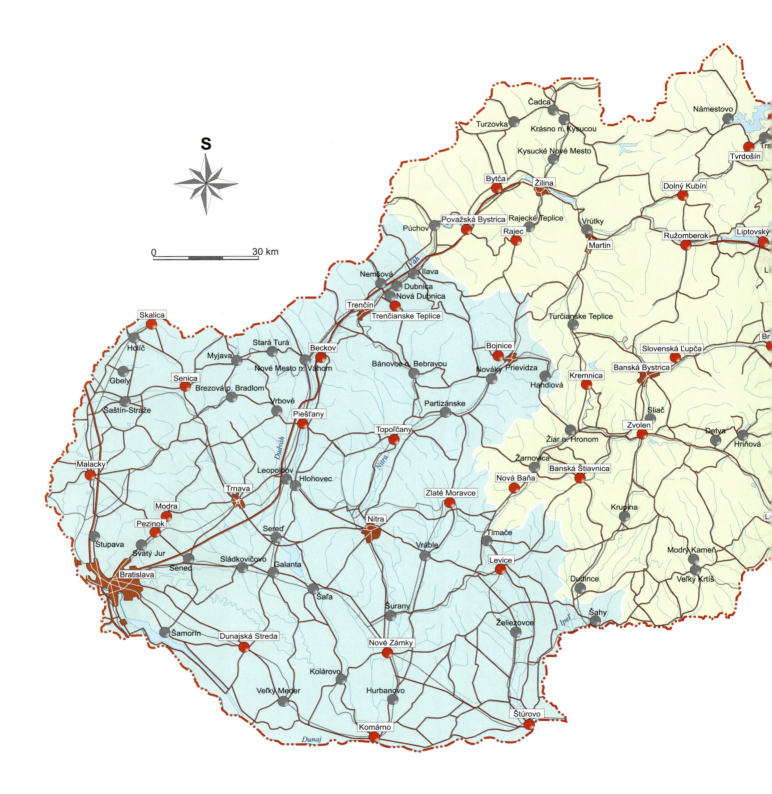